LEADERS OF THE CIVIL WAR ERA

William Tecumseh Sherman

LEADERS OF THE CIVIL WAR ERA

John Brown

Jefferson Davis

Frederick Douglass

Ulysses S. Grant

Stonewall Jackson

Robert E. Lee

Abraham Lincoln

William Tecumseh Sherman

Harriet Beecher Stowe

Harriet Tubman

LEADERS OF THE CIVIL WAR ERA

William Tecumseh Sherman

Rachel Koestler-Grack

CHELSEA HOUSE
PUBLISHERS

An imprint of Infobase Publishing

WILLIAM TECUMSEH SHERMAN

Copyright ©2009 by Infobase Publishing

Chelsea House
An imprint of Infobase Publishing
132 West 31st Street
New York NY 10001

Library of Congress Cataloging-in-Publication Data
Koestler-Grack, Rachel.
William Tecumseh Sherman / Rachel Koestler-Grack.
    p. cm. — (Leaders of the Civil War era)
Includes bibliographical references and index.
ISBN 978-1-60413-300-4 (hardcover : acid-free paper)
1. Sherman, William T. (William Tecumseh), 1820–1891—Juvenile literature. 2. Generals—United States—Biography—Juvenile literature. 3. United States. Army—Biography—Juvenile literature. 4. United States—History—Civil War, 1861–1865—Campaigns—Juvenile literature. I. Title. II. Series.
E467.1.S55K64 2009
355.0092—dc22
[B]   2008045707

Series design by Erik Lindstrom
Cover design by Keith Trego

Printed in the United States of America

Bang KT 10 9 8 7 6 5 4 3 2 1

This book is printed on acid-free paper.

⚔ CONTENTS ⚔

Hard War

At Nashville, Tennessee, Brigadier General William T. Sherman learned that he was to take command of Union forces in the West, from the Mississippi River to the Allegheny Mountains. For the spring campaign of 1864, he planned a march from Chattanooga to Atlanta. In the grand strategy, all Union armies would move together. The forces of General Nathaniel P. Banks would concentrate on Mobile, Alabama. General Benjamin F. Butler would attack Richmond, Virginia, from the south side of the James River. Ulysses S. Grant, the commander of all Union armies, would lead the Army of the Potomac and march against the Confederate forces led by General Robert E. Lee. Sherman and his men would move against General Joseph E. Johnston's army and hit the heart of Georgia.

William Tecumseh Sherman *(center)*, a fierce Union general during the Civil War, was a brilliant military leader and tactician. Though he occasionally failed in battle, his great successes left an indelible mark on the South and contributed greatly to the Union's victory in the war. He is pictured with his generals in 1865.

Sherman was now his own commander. On his shoulders rested the responsibility of success or failure. Only twice before had he led independent commands: in Kentucky, where he had resigned, and in a recent and successful expedition against Meridian, Mississippi, where he had met little opposition. Two years under Henry Halleck and Ulysses S. Grant had strengthened his confidence, however, and taught him to cut straight to the core of battle. In a letter to his wife, Ellen, he wrote, "Think of me, with fifty thousand lives in my hand, with all the anxiety of their families. This load is heavier than you imagine."

As Sherman prepared for the march to Atlanta, he demonstrated his skills as a great military engineer and a master of logistics. This campaign, more than any other military operation during the Civil War, was to emphasize the close relationship between war and technology. Sherman planned to march from Chattanooga through Georgia, along the railroad lines. These railway lines joined in a single route from Louisville, Kentucky, all the way to Atlanta, Georgia. The Nashville and Northwestern road, which before the war had been built from Nashville to Kingston Springs, Tennessee, now had been extended by Union troops to Reynoldsburg, on the Tennessee River. Here, soldiers could transfer freight swiftly from steamboats to boxcars. This continuous hauling of supplies would give his marching men a sort of port on the Tennessee River. The railroad and the river were as much a part of his command as were the bullets for his muskets. Never once did his mules run low on grain.

To make sure that the railroad lines would be safe from Confederate marauders, Sherman developed a precautionary system. A movable railroad base, equipped with repair tools and crews who were trained to rebuild lines and bridges, would help the Yankees to advance without unexpected delays. Sherman trained hundreds of men for railroad maintenance and eventually built up so many experienced construction workers in the army that he was able to order 10,000 soldiers to repair an eight-mile break in the Western and Atlantic railroad line. These men not only served as a talented Union resource during the war, but also were a valuable asset later, in the building of the Union Pacific Railroad.

At the same time, Sherman realized that he could not be bound solely to the railroad system. In enemy country, he would need the freedom to strike out. He therefore organized a horse-and-wagon transportation system that could provide ample supplies without sacrificing mobility. As he developed his plan, he studied the U.S. Census reports for Georgia. From the reports, he learned which areas were the best spots to provide food for his soldiers and animals. He allotted each division and brigade only enough wagons to carry food and ammunition. Every man was to carry along just five days' rations. In addition, one ambulance wagon was assigned to each regiment. The use of tents was strictly forbidden, except to shelter the wounded and to use as headquarter offices.

On May 5, after the Army of the Potomac had crossed the Rapidan River in Virginia and pressed on through the region of that state known as the Wilderness, Sherman began to move his three armies—the Cumberland, under George H. Thomas; the Tennessee, under James B. McPherson; and the Ohio, under John M. Schofield—toward their objective: Atlanta. Mile after mile, as spring turned into scorching summer, Sherman's army swept across Georgia. From Chattanooga to Atlanta, Sherman's men destroyed every town along the way, leaving behind the charred skeletons of buildings and naked ground where fields and farms once stood. On July 17, the troops crossed the Chattahoochee River and began their direct march against Atlanta.

At this point in the campaign, the Confederate government offered valuable assistance to the Union by removing General Johnston from Atlanta and replacing him with the less skillful John B. Hood. Sherman could have outmaneuvered Johnston, but it would have cost extra time and many lives. On July 20, Hood left his entrenchments to fight a losing battle at Peach Tree Creek. He then withdrew to the Confederate defensive lines outside Atlanta. Two days later, both armies were again in the thick of battle. The Union Army of the Tennessee emerged victorious, but the victory came at a high price. General McPherson was killed by the Rebels. Sherman replaced him with Oliver Otis Howard, a West Point graduate with a distinguished record. Weeks passed, and the Yankees gradually surrounded Atlanta, cutting off all rail communication.

On September 1, after more than 100 days of almost continuous fighting, Atlanta at last surrendered. After three years of devastating losses, in the eyes of most Northerners, the victory at Atlanta was the most important Union triumph of 1864. It was, perhaps, the crowning moment in General Sherman's campaign. For the Confederates, the fall of Atlanta meant the loss of Georgia and the death of hope in the South.

"WAR IS WAR"

In Atlanta, Sherman planned stern military measures. He banished all civilians from the city. They could go north or south, but they could not stay. He wanted to transform Atlanta into a pure military garrison, void of any civil influence. In the past months, he had noticed how cities such as Memphis, Vicksburg, Natchez, and New Orleans—all conquered by the Union—needed to be garrisoned by a full division of troops. In a way, success had crippled the army. With each victory, the Union forces lost more detachments—men who were needed in the captured cities to guard and protect the interests of hostile people.

From the beginning, Sherman knew that his orders would stir up a storm of opposition from the enemy. He told Halleck, "If the people raise a howl against my barbarity and cruelty, I will answer that war is war, and not popularity seeking. If they want peace, they and their relatives must stop the war." His aim was to "whip the rebels, to humble their pride, to make them fear and dread" the Union. Sherman referred to his psychological military methods as "hard war." Today, historians call it "total war." Sherman believed that the only way to beat the Rebels was to devastate them so severely that their only choice would be to surrender. However savage he may have seemed, his strategy brought a swift end to a grueling Civil War.

As a military strategist, Sherman was leaps and bounds ahead of his time. He threw off the chains of old methods and traditions, which called for the defeat of the enemy's main army before an invasion of enemy territory. The Civil War was the first conflict fought between modern democracies. Sherman clearly realized that the power of a democracy depends on the strength

92   FRANK LESLIE'S ILLUSTRATED NEWSPAPER.   [Oct. 29, 1864.

Having vowed to "make Georgia howl," Sherman burned and pillaged his way into Atlanta, Georgia. He quickly established his authority and immediately banned all civilians from the city so he could establish a supply location strictly for the military. With Atlanta under his control, Sherman then continued on to conquer Savannah and both North and South Carolina. *Above,* Atlanta residents gather to acquire travel passes that would allow them to leave the area after Sherman's decree of civilian evacuation.

of the people's will even more than it does on the strength of its armies. His grasp of an effective, new type of war has placed him among the top-ranking generals in military history.

Behind the general who led the famous March to the Sea, however, was a boy from a broken family. Under the gruff military commander, there lay a young man who failed at almost every business venture and went bankrupt before the war. Before there was a victorious general, there lived a nearly incompetent commander whom many critics believed to be insane. The rise of William Tecumseh Sherman from tatters to glory is one of the Civil War's greatest stories of bravery, endurance, and determination.

Cump

In the 1820s, Lancaster, Ohio, was a lovely town. A hill in the center of town offered an excellent view of the countryside. To the north of the town rose Mount Pleasant, or as the local Indians called it, Standing Stone; the Kettle Hills dipped and rolled to the south.

Charles Robert Sherman had been a hustling young lawyer in Norwalk, Connecticut. On May 8, 1810, he married Mary Hoyt, a childhood friend. Shortly afterward, he decided that his native state was much too confining for him. In September 1811, Charles and Mary Sherman and their six-month-old son, Charles Taylor, traveled to Lancaster. The couple made the 21-day journey on horseback, with little Charles riding on a pillow between them. They moved into a new, two-story frame house on the corner of an alley and Main Street. In Lancaster,

Charles began to practice law. He covered the court circuit in Marietta and Cincinnati, Ohio, and in Detroit, Michigan. On the circuit, he met Thomas Ewing, a fellow lawyer, and the two men became as close as brothers. The Ewings lived just half a block away from the Shermans, on the summit of a hill. Their grand, white, brick mansion was surrounded by a spacious yard that was dotted with tall shade trees. A high wall with a gate separated the house from the street, and a red-brick sidewalk curved up to the broad front steps.

At about this time, British soldiers crossed the Canadian border and captured both the city of Detroit and the land around Lake Erie to the Maumee River. This invasion marked the beginning of another war between Great Britain and America: the War of 1812. In those days, American Indians still occupied most of Ohio; the American Indians joined the British in their fight against the Americans. The brave and eloquent Shawnee chief Tecumseh organized a grand American Indian confederacy that united many native groups, from the Great Lakes all the way to the Gulf of Mexico. Tecumseh believed that if the American Indians united, they could keep the Americans from invading their homeland. It was not to be, however. Captain Oliver Perry defeated the British on Lake Erie in September 1813, and William Henry Harrison's victory on the Thames River in Ontario, Canada, in October ended the War of 1812. The Americans were triumphant, and they brought down the great Shawnee warrior in that final battle.

Impressed by the Shawnee leader, Charles Sherman vowed to name his second son Tecumseh. The Shermans' first son was named Charles. Just before the war, the Shermans had named a daughter Mary Elizabeth. On December 12, 1814, Mary Sherman gave birth to another son. She insisted, however, that this child be named after her brother James. Two more girls followed: Amelia, in 1816, and Julia, in 1818. Finally, on February 8, 1820, Charles got his wish: another son. This one, he named Tecumseh. The family, however, shortened the name to

Shawnee chief Tecumseh, Sherman's namesake, courageously united several tribes to stand against U.S. expansion and settlement past the Ohio River. One of the most admired American Indian leaders in history, Tecumseh traveled extensively to gather support for an unprecedented alliance. The fearless warrior later died in the War of 1812.

"Cump." During the next decade, the Shermans had five more children: Lampson Parker, John, Susan, Hoyt, and Frances, or Fanny. This brought the total to a bustling 11 children.

As the size of his family increased, Charles Sherman's professional life took a downward turn. For a while, he collected tax payments on items such as liquor, salt, and sugar. All of the payments were paid with notes from the local bank—the only currency available in Ohio. In July 1817, the federal government refused to accept these notes. Instead, the government demanded the banknotes of the recently chartered Bank of the United States. Sherman's deputies, who held large amounts of local notes, took a heavy loss. Assuming the obligation for his deputies, Sherman mortgaged all of his property. He spent the rest of his life trying to pay off the debt. Things took a turn for the better in 1823, when the state legislature appointed Charles Sherman one of the four judges of the Ohio Supreme Court.

Then, on a bright June morning in 1829, tragedy struck the family. Charles Sherman, who had been seriously ill with typhoid fever, died, leaving Mary to shoulder his incredible debt. Unable to support her many children, Mary was forced to split the family apart. She sent the children away to live with relatives and friends. Fortunately, the oldest boy, Charles, was off studying law in Mansfield, Ohio, and the oldest girl, Elizabeth, was engaged to be married. Mary still had to find homes for the other nine children, however. Thomas Ewing offered to take one of the boys to live with his family. When he stopped by the Shermans' house to pick up the child, he asked Elizabeth which one of the boys would be his. "Oh, Mr. Ewing," Elizabeth said, as recounted in James M. Merrill's *William Tecumseh Sherman*, "take Cump. He's the brightest."

That day, nine-year-old Tecumseh moved in with the Ewing family. The Ewings treated Tecumseh as their own son, even though they never formally adopted him. An ardent Catholic, Maria Ewing sometimes invited a traveling Catholic priest to stay at the house. On one of his visits, Maria asked the priest to baptize Tecumseh, even though he already had been baptized in the Presbyterian faith. Before the ceremony, one of the Ewing children ran down the block to make sure it was all right with Mary Sherman. She had no objections. The priest performed the baptism in the Ewings' front parlor. Because it was St.

William's Day, Cump was baptized William. From that day forward, Cump always signed his name William T. Sherman.

Cump became close friends with Philemon Ewing, who was just eight months younger. In the winter, the boys had snowball fights and went sliding on the frozen river. In the summer, they spent the afternoons fishing, swimming, and roaming the wooded hills along the riverbanks. Some days, they sat on stumps near the docks and watched canal boats chug in and out with their cargoes. Phil and Cump attended a school run by two brothers, Samuel and Mark Howe. John Sherman, Cump's younger brother, remembered William as a quiet and steady student who was moved by sympathy and affection for others. The Ewings also made the boys take French lessons at an elite and expensive French school. One morning, when Phil and Cump were supposed to get up for school, the boys suddenly acted sick and said that they wanted to stay in bed. Thomas Ewing, wise to their prank, decided to play a joke on them. If they were sick, he told them, they each would have to take a dose of bitter medicine. Not wanting Ewing to find out that they were faking, the boys swallowed the horrible concoction. Afterward, Ewing roared with laughter. The boys, realizing that they had just been punished, forced out a light chuckle as well. After that, Ewing did not force the boys to study French.

In 1831, two years after Cump went to live with the Ewings, Thomas Ewing was elected to the United States Senate on the Whig ticket. The Whig Party, which included such notable members of Congress as Daniel Webster and Henry Clay, disagreed with the popular, Democratic movement that supported President Andrew Jackson. Since the late 1820s, the state of South Carolina had been threatening to nullify the tariff laws of the United States, which the state's representatives claimed favored Northern manufacturers at the expense of Southern cotton and tobacco growers. Senator Robert Y. Hayne of South Carolina suggested an alliance of Southern

After the death of his father, Sherman was sent to live with the family of Thomas Ewing *(above)*. Elected to the U.S. Senate soon after Sherman's arrival into the family, Ewing continued to provide the boy with a home, a family, and an education by enrolling him in the U.S. Military Academy at West Point. Later, the two men shared similar views and were strong supporters of preserving the Union.

states and Western states to push for low tariffs and cheap land. The standoff became known as the Nullification Crisis.

Senator Daniel Webster of Massachusetts defended the position of the Northeastern states. He accused South Carolina of being "anti-Union." Webster argued that the Constitution was a compact of the American people, not merely of the states. Through his strong and clear defense of nationalism, Webster made the states' rights position favored by South Carolina seem close to treason. Webster's stance was effective in bringing a South-West alliance to an abrupt halt.

Thomas Ewing supported Webster's policies. Ewing lashed out at South Carolina's ideas about the supremacy of the state. In one speech, he asserted that nullification amounted to a declaration of war. "The allegiance which a citizen owes to his State," he said, as reported in Merrill's *William Tecumseh Sherman*, "[must] yield to that paramount allegiance which he owes to the Union." In other words, Ewing believed that Americans should pledge their loyalty first to the Union and second to their state.

Cump Sherman grew up accepting many of his foster father's political principles concerning the Union, the Constitution, and the law. Senator Ewing was also a strong supporter of the abolition of slavery in the District of Columbia. When he realized that the issue might disrupt the nation, however, he decided that preserving the Union was more important than outlawing slavery in the nation's capital.

In the fall of 1834 and the spring of 1835, 15-year-old Sherman was one of four boys selected from the Howe school to work as rodmen—surveyor's assistants—on a surveying party. On this job, Sherman helped mark routes from the Great Ohio Canal south through Lancaster and the Hocking Valley to the Ohio River. Waking before daylight and working a long day, he earned a silver dollar for each day's work.

When William Sherman was 16, Thomas Ewing helped to fulfill Charles Sherman's wish for his son: that he attend the United States Military Academy at West Point, New York. As a U.S. senator, Ewing had some pull in getting Sherman accepted. In late May of 1836, Sherman left Lancaster for West Point. Before he left, he said a long and tearful good-bye to his mother, Mary.

WEST POINT CADET

On arriving at West Point, Sherman and the other freshmen, called plebes, picked up their bags and trudged up the wind-

THE LONG GRAY LINE

The United States Military Academy at West Point is also known as USMA, West Point, "The Point," or, when speaking of college athletics, Army. It was the first United States military post built after the Declaration of Independence. The Point was first occupied as a fort in 1778; this makes it the oldest continuously occupied military post in U.S. history. Formally established by Thomas Jefferson in 1802, the academy stands on a scenic overlook of the Hudson River, about 50 miles north of New York City. Covering more than 16,000 acres of land, it is one of the largest school campuses in the world. The Point's unique facilities include a ski slope and an artillery range in addition to the academic buildings and sports facilities found on a typical university campus.

Students at the academy are referred to as cadets. About 1,200 new cadets enter the Point on Reception Day each year. West Point trains cadets in four critical areas: intellectual, physical, military, and moral-ethical. Cadets refer to the four-year process as the "West Point Experience." The foundation of the ethical code at West

ing road that led to the barracks and other academy buildings. At the adjutant's office, Sherman signed official papers and paid his tuition. From there, he dropped his bags off at his barracks. On that first afternoon, all plebes were interviewed by the superintendent and issued one arithmetic book, one lamp, one bucket, one broom, and a set of blankets. Back at the barracks, Sherman fell asleep while paging through the West Point book of regulations. Suddenly, a drumroll startled him awake. He heard the command, "Turn out, new cadets!"

Point is broken down to its basic elements in the academy's motto: "Duty, Honor, Country." Cadets also develop ethically by adhering to the Cadet Honor Code, which states, "A cadet will not lie, cheat, steal, or tolerate those who do." On graduation, each cadet is awarded a bachelor of science degree and a commission in the United States Army. Every year, the U.S. Army commissions more than 900 West Point graduates as second lieutenants. Today, these men and women make up 25 percent of new second lieutenants in the U.S. Army. They serve on active duty for a minimum of five years.

Cadets and graduates are known as "The Long Gray Line" because of the color of the cadets' uniforms and the unbroken line, or lineage, of West Point graduates. The 4,000 members of the Corps of Cadets represent every state in the United States and several foreign countries. West Point trains more United States Army officers than any other single institution, and many of America's most distinguished generals have been West Point graduates, including William T. Sherman.

Sherman and the other cadets tumbled out of their rooms and rumbled down the stairs. "Fall in!" an officer yelled. The plebes lined up in formation and marched around the corner of the South Barracks to watch the evening parade. Later, Sherman recalled, "I felt the beauty of Military parade and show—the fine music—the old cadets marching by companies, stepping as one man, all forming in line." He was captivated by the roar of the evening gun and by the flag that waved majestically in the evening breeze. He decided at that moment, "My highest ambition was to be a cadet."

The new cadets were drilled three times a day: shortly after sunrise, at ten in the morning, and at four in the afternoon. Infantry drill, artillery drill, and dress parades dominated the day. The rest of the day was spent in class or in study. Under the strict rules, cadets were confined to their rooms the rest of the time, except for a few minutes after each meal. Sherman once wrote to Phil Ewing, who was studying law at Oxford College in England, "I wish to God we could be as independent as you, that is recite when we please, and study when we please, and do whatever we please, but no, drill & recite all day . . . which means study all night or take the consequences." At West Point, the course work was so strenuous that only those cadets with outstanding ability managed to stay in school. Those who could not keep up were dismissed. In less than three years, Sherman's class was reduced from 115 men to 43.

Although Sherman took pride in being a cadet, he was restless, independent, full of energy, and often impatient with regulations and bumbling superiors. Occasionally, he even took part in troublesome pranks. Right away, he racked up some demerits. He earned his first official demerit for not carrying the butt of his musket far enough back at parade. Some of his other demerits were for soiled clothing (cadets had to keep their uniforms spotless at all times) and for being absent at roll call, drill, or parade. Fellow cadet William S. Rosecrans recalled that Sherman "was always ready for a lark and usually had a grease spot on his pants from clandestine night feasts."

The major goal of West Point was to turn out soldiers—officers who could fight hard and obey orders implicitly. Despite his mischievous behavior, Sherman proved to be a strong and capable cadet. On July 1, 1840, William Tecumseh Sherman graduated sixth in his class of 43. He would have finished third, but his demerits, which averaged 150 a year (a student with more than 200 a year got expelled), dragged him down three notches.

After graduation, Second Lieutenant Sherman returned home to Lancaster for a dull summer vacation. The boredom was quickly replaced by his first experience on active duty, however. He received orders that the Third Artillery of Company A was to report for duty at Fort Columbus, in New York Harbor, on September 20. Soon, Sherman was on his way to Florida and the Seminole War.

From Coast
to Coast

Before he reported to Fort Columbus, Sherman stopped by West Point. There, he spent the night at the academy's West Point Hotel. The next day, after morning call to quarters, he went up to the barracks to visit some of his old friends. For about half an hour, he relaxed in the room of one of the cadets. Although Sherman knew that it was against regulations to be there, he figured that, as a second lieutenant, the academy's rules did not apply to him. As he left the barracks, he noticed Lieutenant George G. Waggaman, then the adjutant of the academy, briskly walking toward him. The lieutenant placed Sherman under arrest for visiting cadets during study hours. Shocked, Sherman tried to argue with the lieutenant, but it was no use.

In an "arrested" military order, Sherman continued to Fort Columbus. He handed his legal papers to the commanding officer, Major Justin Dimick, who paged through them. The major glanced up at Sherman. "So you are under arrest?" he asked. Sherman nodded. "Well, it looks like a small matter," Dimick said, an evaluation with which Sherman wholeheartedly agreed. "But as the arrest comes from Major Delafield," Dimick continued, as quoted in Merrill's *William Tecumseh Sherman*, "it must be respected."

Sherman was ordered to report for duty at ten the following morning. By that time, all of his West Point comrades in the Third Artillery already had been assigned to command various recruit companies. Because Sherman was under arrest, however, he could not yet assume a command position. At once, he wrote a sincere apology to Major Delafield, agreeing that his conduct was inappropriate. Satisfied, the major recommended that Sherman be restored to duty and that the matter be put to rest.

By mid-October of 1840, Sherman had arrived in St. Augustine, Florida. From there, he headed southward to join Company A at Fort Pierce. Built on a sandbank 20 feet from a lagoon, the fort consisted of log huts that formed three sides of a rectangle; the fourth side was open to the water. The small companies of A and F were garrisoned there, waiting to begin operations against the Seminole Indians. A war of countless skirmishes in marshy terrain, the Seminole War had been dragging on since 1835. The Seminole were trying to defend their homeland against white settlers; the American government wanted the American Indians to give up their land and move onto government reservations. Because Florida is crisscrossed by rivers, streams, and swamps, the battles were difficult. Villages, built on hammocks (raised dry patches of land), were well hidden behind thick foliage, including grasses and

Sherman's first military experience came when he reported for duty in the Seminole War. Fought in the wilderness of the Florida Everglades, the U.S. Army struggled to capture all the Seminole in the area and never successfully ended the war. The conflict ended after seven years without a peace treaty or a clear winner. Most Seminole relocated to Oklahoma while a few stalwart members remained in the swamps.

palmetto trees. The U.S. Army was in Florida to flush out and destroy the Seminole.

In the spring of 1841, the Seminole chief Coacoochee, known as Wild Cat, rode to Tampa Bay to tell the commanding general there, Walker K. Armistead, that his people were weary of war. Coacoochee said that the Seminole would immigrate to American Indian territory, in present-day Oklahoma, if the Americans would give them time and assistance. Glad to hear of a possible end to the war, Armistead issued Wild Cat a safe-conduct pass that allowed the chief to enter any military post on the Florida coast. At the forts, the commanding officers would do whatever they could to help Wild Cat gather the Seminole people together.

Not long after, Major Childs at Fort Pierce learned that Wild Cat was nearby. He ordered Sherman to take 12 men on horseback, find the Seminole chief, and bring him back to the fort. Just five miles away, Sherman found a group of Seminole warriors. Wild Cat was one of them. At Fort Pierce, Wild Cat told Major Childs that in one moon—a month—his people would be ready to move to the reservation. He then left the fort, taking with him an ample supply of flour, sugar, and coffee.

During the next few weeks, small parties of Seminole trickled into the fort. The local commanders mistrusted the American Indians, however. The Americans feared that they would revolt and unleash a deadly rampage. Childs asked Colonel William Jenkins Worth, who had taken over as commander in chief of the Florida Army, for the authority to revoke Coacoochee's safe-conduct pass. Worth went one step further: He commanded Childs to capture Wild Cat. The next time Wild Cat showed up at Fort Pierce, the soldiers seized him and his warriors and clamped them in iron shackles. The following day, Lieutenant Colonel William Gates, commander of the Third Artillery, marched into Fort Pierce with an additional company. Seeing the imprisoned chief, he ordered the soldiers to transport Wild Cat to New Orleans and from there to the Indian Territory beyond. When Colonel Worth got the news about Gates's orders, he was furious. Worth had planned to use the captured chief to persuade other Seminole to surrender. He reprimanded Gates for issuing orders without permission and had Wild Cat brought back to Tampa.

Even with the capture of Wild Cat, the Seminole War was not at an end. Like many of the other soldiers, Sherman grew tired of the dragged-out war. The more he saw of the war, the more he believed that there was no end to it unless the American Indians surrendered. Sherman realized that this war could not be fought using the maneuvers he had learned in field manuals at West Point. His dedication to his military duty never faltered, however. In a letter to Phil Ewing, as quoted in Merrill's *William Tecumseh Sherman*, he wrote,

> Some old fogies . . . have demanded to be relieved from duty in Florida. . . . A soldier to demand to be relieved from the very spot where his duty calls him is an absurdity and I assure you that however anxious officers of this regiment are to go north after six years service here, yet not one except the colonel [Gates] would think of such a thing as demanding it. . . . We've all made up our minds to stay here until the end of the war, when that will be God only knows.

For Sherman, the stay in the swamps surrounding Fort Pierce was short lived. After being promoted to first lieutenant in November 1841, he was transferred to Picolata, Florida, where he took command of a detachment of Company G. Located along the banks of the St. Johns River, the old settlement of Picolata was quite an improvement over Fort Pierce. The fort consisted of a large frame house, barracks, outhouses, guardhouses, and stables, all surrounded by beautiful wooded countryside. Just 18 miles from St. Augustine—the oldest town in the United States, established by the Spanish in 1565—Sherman could maintain a regular social life. He was impressed by Picolata's charming plaza, with its quaint Spanish villas, and the narrow, winding streets lined by snugly built houses with jutting balconies.

At Picolata, Sherman also enjoyed leisure time. He spent many afternoons playing cards or dice. In the evenings, he often attended parties, dances, and masquerades. It was nothing like the dancing in the North. Here, ladies waltzed all night without tiring, gliding across the floor in slow, fluid motion.

Soon, however, Sherman was shuffled off to another post. After a year at Picolata, the entire 3rd Artillery was ordered to garrison posts along the Gulf of Mexico. Sherman's outfit, Company G, reported to Fort Morgan, at the mouth of

Mobile Bay, in Alabama. On March 8, 1842, the steamship *Cincinnati* pulled alongside a small dock near Fort Morgan, and the men of Company G disembarked. Fort Morgan was a series of heavy casemates—armored enclosures for big guns—and arches arranged as strongholds, covered with thick, sharp wire.

Once again, post routine was monotonous and uneventful. The officers found their only excitement in the city of Mobile, where the streets were lined with fine hotels and shops. The officers' uniforms were passports to the best and most expensive homes in town. Sherman and his men were invited to balls, art galleries, and the theater.

In Mobile, Sherman looked up his cousin Mrs. Bull, the former Cornelia Pyle. She, her husband, and their three children lived in one of the magnificent homes of Mobile. Sherman found the Bulls' family life a perfect paradise, yet he had no intention of seeking marriage himself. He doubted that the army was the proper place for a married man, unless that man found a wife who was willing to forsake a constant home and the comforts of a civilized life. According to Sherman, the frequent changes that officers were required to make would destroy the comfort that a family should possess.

In June, Sherman's company made another move, this time to Fort Moultrie, in South Carolina. The fort stood along the Atlantic coast, on Sullivan's Island, overlooking the ocean and Charleston Harbor. Just as at Fort Morgan, the military routine was not strenuous. Each morning, Sherman woke to reveille and drilled at sunrise. After breakfast, the officers took part in a dress parade, followed by the changing of the guard. Beyond their obligatory guard duty, officers had much leisure time. To pass the hours, Sherman took up painting, mostly landscapes and portraits. At times, he found himself so drawn into his artistic world that it almost hurt to set down his brush.

Walking through the streets of nearby Charleston was like roaming the streets of a fairy-tale city. The town was dotted with luxurious mansions, all of which had been built by slave labor. The forced work of thousands of slaves was the source of all wealth in the South, and the slaves themselves were considered valuable possessions. They were, in fact, the most important commodities in the South. The Southern economy depended on slavery to thrive and survive.

In the 1840s, Sherman did not strongly oppose slavery. From what he saw, the slaves were treated well and with kindness. "I am no advocate for slavery as a means of wealth or national advancement," Sherman told Phil Ewing in a letter, "yet at the same time I know that the idea of oppression and tyranny that some people consider as the necessary accompaniment of slavery is a delusion of their own brain." Many slave owners did not treat their slaves kindly, however. Although Sherman witnessed runaway slaves being captured in the swamps and hauled back into bondage, he saw little wrong with slavery as an institution. He believed that Northern abolitionists—men and women who hid runaway slaves and protested against slavery, sometimes violently—were dangerous troublemakers. Sherman thought that slavery would die out on its own one day and that there was no reason to push the issue.

During the winter of 1842–1843, Sherman received invitations to balls, operas, picnics, boating parties, and the horse races. He found Charleston balls dreadfully boring compared with those in St. Augustine. For one thing, the dancing of the local girls could not compare with that of the graceful Spanish girls of Florida. At one of these balls, however, Sherman met one of the prettiest young ladies in Charleston, Mary Lamb. He escorted her to the opera and to the theater and even rode side by side with her in a carriage—something that, at the time, a man and woman did only when they were in a serious relationship. When people in Charleston started to gossip about the couple, Sherman fumed. "I had no idea that people here were so foolish as to raise and circulate rumors of that kind,"

When Sherman was adopted into the Ewing family, he became close friends with Ellen Ewing and remained in contact with her while he was away with the military. Despite his early romances with other women and his vows to remain a bachelor, Sherman fell in love with Ellen and the two were later married.

he told Phil Ewing. "I'll *never marry*. . . . If I ever do, be sure to knock out my brains."

During a trip home to Lancaster in the summer of 1843, Sherman began to rethink his feelings about marriage. He started to look at Phil Ewing's sister Ellen in a new way. He noticed her delicate features, her penetrating blue eyes, and the soft black hair that she pulled back over her ears. During his time serving in the South, Sherman had kept in close contact with Ellen Ewing, but only as a friend. That summer, he spent much of his time with her, and the two of them fell deeply in love.

Back at Fort Moultrie, Sherman could hardly stand to be away from her. In one letter, he wrote, "I would give years of my life if you could have been here this evening to hear Mrs. Keyes sing, have a sociable chat with Mrs. Hawkins, eat some of her mince pies, drink whiskey punch." Then, revealing his romantic side, Sherman told her that he wished they could stand together on the shore, watching "the moon rise slowly from her watery bed."

During his posting at Fort Moultrie, Sherman's service was interrupted by missions to other parts of the South. He was sent to Key West, Florida, to check into the conduct of a captain there; to Augusta, Georgia, to examine the books of the arsenal; and to locations in North Carolina and Louisiana to deal with other issues. One trip through Georgia and Alabama took him over the very ground where, 20 years later, in the turmoil of the Civil War, he fought some of his best campaigns.

In February 1844, Colonel Sylvester Churchill, the U.S. inspector general, asked that Lieutenant Sherman be sent to Marietta, Georgia, to examine claims submitted by militiamen from Georgia and Alabama for horses lost during their service in Florida. Sherman was surprised but delighted that he had been singled out by one of the best officers in the service. After six weeks in Marietta, Churchill took Sherman and his party of officers across the mountains to Bellefont, Alabama. The trip and, specifically, the route they took proved to be valuable for Sherman. Even 20 years later, he recalled perfectly the water, the ground, and the mountain ranges of the area. All of it became vital knowledge for a successful commander.

By June, Sherman was back at Fort Moultrie, facing complications in his romantic relationship with Ellen Ewing. Having kept their relationship secret up until this point, the young couple decided it was time to tell Thomas and Maria Ewing that they planned to get married. Maria immediately approved of the match, but Thomas was less than thrilled. He did not want his daughter to become an army wife. He tried to convince Sherman to give up the military and find a respectable job as a civilian. Sherman refused to leave the army. In his opinion, it was the only profession for which he was suited, and he thought it would be silly to take up a new career at this point in his life. At last, Thomas Ewing eased up on Sherman, and the couple began to make wedding plans. In November 1845, Sherman wrote Ellen a letter in which he suggested that they settle in Alabama. According to Sherman, that state offered some of the most beautiful land in the United States. He even promised to look into job possibilities there the following spring.

Rumors of war with Mexico brought Sherman's plans to a screeching halt. Less than a month after Sherman's letter to Ellen, Congress voted to annex Texas. This action set the stage for the Mexican War. In March 1846, President James Polk sent troops to secure the Texas border. Braxton Bragg's company at Fort Moultrie received orders to report to New Orleans, where they were to be converted into a mounted force and decked out for war. Eager to see battle, Sherman hoped for orders to Texas as well. Instead, the War Department sent him to organize recruits in Pittsburgh, Pennsylvania. Just as he was settling in at his new post, news arrived that a Mexican force had crossed the Rio Grande and attacked an American patrol. At once,

Congress declared war on Mexico, and 50,000 troops were dispatched to fight.

For Sherman, it was almost excruciating to be stuck with recruit duty when a war was being waged elsewhere. He sent a letter to his superior officer requesting a transfer to the field, but he never received a reply. Sherman decided to personally transfer a group of 30 recruits to Newport, Kentucky, in the hope that he would be ordered west from there. In Newport, instead of being praised for his enthusiasm, he received a firm scolding and was sent back to Pittsburgh. There, in his quarters, a new set of orders awaited him. As soon as possible, he was to go to New York to report to Captain Christopher Q. Tompkins of Company F for duty. He also received a letter from an old West Point classmate, Edward Ord, telling him that Company F was going to set sail at once for California. At that time, California was part of Mexico.

"Ordered to California by sea around Cape Horn!" he wrote to Ellen. "Indeed it is so great an event that I cannot realize it in its full force." He would not be on the fighting front, but at least he could feel like a pioneer in a far-off country. No doubt, leaving Ellen so far behind was the hardest part. He told her brother Phil, "But such is the glory of war." In September 1846, instead of settling with a wife in Alabama as he had expected, he was aboard the naval ship *Lexington*, rounding South America's Cape Horn and heading for the battlefields of the Mexican War.

CALIFORNIA

The Mexican War of 1846–1848 inspired its fair share of American opposition. Years later, General Ulysses S. Grant, who first gained fame in this war, described it as "one of the most unjust ever waged by a stronger against a weaker nation." Still, after a year and a half of fighting, the United States grew nearly one-fourth larger. Few Americans argued with the outcome:

the addition to the map of the United States of New Mexico, California, and what are today the states of Nevada and Utah, plus parts of Colorado and Wyoming.

The trouble began in 1845, when Texas was annexed to the United States. Texas had won its independence from Mexico in 1836. When Texas wanted to join the Union, Mexico resisted, declaring that this action would start a war. The United States ignored the threat and annexed Texas as its twenty-eighth and largest state. The chief source of conflict was a disagreement over the location of the border. According to Mexico, its northern border ran along the Nueces River. The United States claimed that the border was the Rio Grande. In March 1846, General Zachary Taylor moved 3,500 troops to Camp Texas, in present-day Brownsville, Texas. On May 1, Camp Texas was attacked by 6,000 Mexican fighters under General Mariano Arista. General Taylor's army drove them off. The U.S. Army quickly won two other battles, at Palo Alto and Resaca de la Palma. Then, on May 13, the United States officially declared war on Mexico.

On January 26, 1847, after 198 days at sea, the *Lexington* dropped anchor in Monterey Bay, off the California coast. From the deck, Sherman gazed at the shoreline. Whitewashed adobe houses dotted the lush green landscape against a backdrop of tall oaks and dark pines. The town of Monterey curved around the sparkling blue bay like a crescent moon. Immediately, Sherman was captivated by the California coast. By the time he arrived, American forces already had seized and occupied Monterey, the former capital of Mexico's Alta California. Although some locals still lived in the city, it was nearly deserted.

In 1847, California was what today would be considered undeveloped land. Much of its expanse of 150,000 square miles was accessible only by foot or on horseback. Probably no more than 25,000 people lived there, including the American Indians who made up more than half of the population. A mere 1,000

Americans were in California, and most of those had just arrived on the *Lexington*.

At Monterey, Colonel Richard Mason was in command. He appointed Sherman assistant adjutant general for the 10th Military District and named Henry Halleck secretary of state. In their new posts, Sherman attended to all military affairs and Halleck attended to civil issues. The officers moved into the customs house, a large, two-story building that overlooked the port.

At once, the colonel began to lay down the law. He declared that military rules superseded civil ones. He had little patience for the local legal practices and customs that had been set up by the former government. Hangings were a case in point. From time to time, as a man was hanged, the rope broke or the knot slipped. The locals interpreted this sort of thing as a divine miracle, and the criminal was freed. When such a miracle happened twice in one day, the local priest rushed to Mason to report the double wonder and to ask for the release of the prisoners. Mason stiffly answered, "The prisoners were condemned to be hung by the neck until dead, and when this sentence had been executed the knot slipping business might be looked into."

Sherman had a great deal of respect and admiration for Mason. "Colonel Mason is an excellent man, well suited for his office, a little severe for civilians, but just and determined," he wrote to Ellen. Years later, an officer under Sherman may have uttered these same words about him. Sherman's time with Mason served as a sort of apprenticeship. Under the colonel, he learned how to deal with a whole range of problems that arose when troops tried to control a hostile area—problems that Sherman dealt with later, in the Civil War. Like Mason, Sherman based his command on the laws of war.

With fewer than 1,000 troops at his disposal, Mason dispatched small forces to various posts throughout the city. He believed that it was important to keep a show of troops, no matter how small the number. In December 1847, the officers worried about a possible rebellion. At that time, there was fighting to the south, in American-held Mazatlan, and some people thought that the war might spread from Lower to Upper California. Soon after, however, the threat diminished.

As assistant adjutant general, Sherman prepared endless reports from the colonel to be sent to Washington, as well as written orders and correspondence. Six days of the week, Sherman sat hunched over a table in the customs house, thumbing through stacks of papers. He carefully read through each report. Then he grabbed a piece of blank paper and began to scrawl on it with his rapid, slanted writing. If Colonel Mason appeared with yet another stack of papers, Sherman accepted the work with a dutiful nod. Sometimes, however, all the mind-numbing paperwork exhausted him. He wrote to Ellen, "I have been bending over a table till my head aches almost to bursting."

Swamped with duties, Sherman missed Ellen desperately. Back East, he had received frequent letters from her. In California, however, mail delivery was slow and irregular. As soon as he arrived in California, he wrote Ellen a letter. He had to wait two months, however, before a departing ship could carry the letter back East. Similarly, Ellen mailed a letter to Sherman in October 1846. He did not receive it until the following April. Ellen, meanwhile, was having second thoughts about their engagement. She suffered from chronic pain and swelling in her neck, which caused her extreme fatigue. At times, fearing that she could pass her ailments on to her children, she felt that it would be best for her to remain single. Sherman would not hear of it. In his mind, there was only one woman for him—Ellen Ewing.

Sherman did, however, become bothered by Ellen's extreme religious beliefs. On one occasion, she wrote to Sherman about her bother Hugh, who was not doing well at West Point. She believed that his troubles were the result of a lack of morals at the academy—a lack that had weakened Hugh's Christian faith.

In response, Sherman sternly told Ellen that it was folly to suggest that the state of Hugh's soul was hindering his chances of graduation. "That has nothing to do with his want of industry and enterprise," he scolded. "Don't write to him as you do to me about the sinfulness of war and all that."

In California, Sherman's health suffered as well. He fell victim to asthma and bouts of violent coughs. During the winter of 1847–1848, he also became depressed. He was overloaded with work, isolated from his dearest Ellen, and banished from the fame that came to soldiers active in the battlefield. In the spring, however, some nearby excitement cheered his spirits: Gold was discovered at Sutter's Mill.

John Sutter, the owner of the mill, sent samples to Colonel Mason in Monterey to confirm that they were, indeed, gold. The colonel called in Sherman to help him test the samples. Because no acids were available to do a hot acid test, Sherman tried a malleability, or softness, test: He bit down on a nugget and then struck it with a hammer. The nugget dented. This meant that it was soft—a property of gold. Colonel Mason let Sutter know that the metal found on his property was, in fact, true gold.

At first, Sutter tried to keep his discovery a secret, but word quickly leaked out. As news spread eastward, men throughout the United States dropped what they were doing and hurried overland to California. About 100,000 men rushed to the gold fields. Sensational stories filled newspapers across the country. One man, panning at a place called Hudson's Gulch, sifted 244 ounces of gold from a single pan. At Sierra City, another digger unearthed a 148-pound nugget. To many Americans, it seemed like the legendary golden land of El Dorado had been discovered.

In June 1848, Sherman and Mason visited the site of the gold strike. Tents and shacks littered the landscape. Gold seekers swarmed across the countryside, and the streams were crowded with panners. By the fall of 1850, there were about 250,000 people in California—10 times the population that was there in 1846, when Sherman's company landed at Monterey Bay. Even soldiers were not immune to gold fever. Many abandoned their posts for a chance to strike it rich. At one point during 1848, the number of active servicemen shrank to just 50.

Sherman, too, was tempted by the idea of finding a fortune. He was not enticed by the prospect of panning for gold,

EL DORADO

After the Gold Rush in 1849, prospectors—people in search of gold—hurried to California, hoping to discover a piece of the treasure. El Dorado—"the golden one" in Spanish—is a legend that began with the story of a South American tribal chief who would sprinkle himself with gold dust and dive into a lake in the Andes Mountains. Over the years, rumors arose that the legend of El Dorado was actually a place, a kingdom of tremendous treasure and wealth, ruled by this legendary golden king.

In the 1500s, South American towns and their treasures fell to the Spanish conquistadores. However, the Spaniards soon realized that—even though the natives had large quantities of gold in their possession—there were no golden cities, nor even rich mines. The natives obtained all their gold in trade. Still, the Spanish heard stories of El Dorado from captured natives, and the legend lived on. Eventually, the name of El Dorado became a metaphor for any place where wealth could be rapidly acquired—such as in California. In fact, an area of California was named El Dorado County.

The discovery of gold at Sutter's Mill gripped the nation in gold rush fever and men flocked to the region, hoping to find their fortune. Sherman, who was working as an assistant to Colonel Richard Mason in San Francisco at the time, helped confirm that the identity of the first nuggets discovered in the region were, in fact, gold. *Above*, prospectors panning for gold during the California Gold Rush.

however. It looked to be a lot of work for a less-than-certain payout. He believed that a real fortune could be made by selling supplies to eager gold diggers. In the fall of 1848, Sherman and some of his men decided to make a little money. Sherman claimed that the colonel would not mind. Sherman realized that he and his men could buy supplies in Monterey and sell them at the digging sites for four times as much as they had paid for them. A thirsty miner with plenty of gold dust would be more than willing to trade an ounce of gold—worth $18 at the U.S. Mint—for an ounce of whiskey. For a while, Sherman and another officer—William Warner—operated a store for miners. Sherman wrote a letter to a friend back East: If the friend could send $10,000 worth of shoes, blankets, and clothing to California, Sherman could sell the goods for a handsome profit.

Colonel Mason could see that he had a massive problem on his hands. Just as he was about to take strong action against his disorderly men, however, the war with Mexico ended. As part of the peace agreement, California became a territory of the United States. Because California was destined to enter the Union as a free state—a state in which slavery was illegal—the territory immediately was caught up in the growing national controversy about slavery.

The debate was settled, at least temporarily, with the Compromise of 1850. Under the terms of this congressional legislation, California was admitted to the Union as a free state, and the rest of the land acquired in the Mexican War—present-day Utah, Colorado, Arizona, and New Mexico—could be admitted as slave states. This compromise was created to keep Southern states from seceding, or leaving, the Union to form their own separate government, something that they had been threatening to do if all of the new territory was designated as free.

In February 1849, Colonel Mason received orders to return to Washington. General Persifer Smith became commander of the Division of the Pacific, and General Bennet Riley became military governor of California. Before Mason left, one of his last official acts as commander was to approve Sherman's application for leave. With it, he gave his young protégé a tremendous compliment. "If there is an officer in the whole army who . . . merits an indulgence," he said, "it is Lieutenant W.T. Sherman." Unfortunately, Mason's praise did not help Sherman. General Smith refused to grant his leave, probably because he needed Sherman to help him take over his new command.

The rejection did not go well with Sherman. He wrote to Ellen that he was tempted to resign, but it might take two years for the necessary paperwork to go through. Sensing his lieutenant's frustration, on May 15, Smith authorized a brief, 60-day leave for Sherman. Sherman hoped to build up some savings during his leave, most likely by working as a surveyor. His friend James Ord had made $3,000 in six weeks doing surveying work in the Los Angeles area. Such opportunities abounded in California. All Sherman needed was the time to take advantage of them.

In June, Sherman learned that Colonel Mason had been promoted to brigadier general as a reward for his work in California. Sherman, his able assistant, had been over-looked. This time, Sherman decided to do something rash. He resigned from the army—out of self-respect, he claimed. More likely, however, his resignation had much to do with the fact that he and Ellen were planning to get married soon. If he stayed in the army, he would need a promotion to support a family. When Sherman returned from his leave, however, he found that nothing had been done about his resignation. General Smith simply had set the letter aside, wanting to talk to Sherman in person. Smith encouraged Sherman about his prospects for promotion. He promised to send Sherman back East later in the year to deliver dispatches to Winfield Scott, the commanding general of the army. For the time being, Smith agreed to make Sherman one of his aides-de-camp, offi-cers who had much free time. In this position, Sherman could continue to work as a surveyor in his spare time. This allowed him to make several thousand dollars.

At the end of the year, as promised, General Smith sent Sherman back to the East. On New Year's Day, 1850, almost three years after the day he arrived in California, Sherman sailed out of Monterey Bay. At the time, he scarcely imagined that he would return one day.

Juggling Family
and Finances

Sherman arrived in New York by steamship just a month after he left California. Much had changed while he was away. The Whigs had triumphed in the election of 1848, and General Zachary Taylor was now president. Shortly after landing in New York, Sherman learned that General Winfield Scott, the commander who had conquered Mexico City, was in New York. At once, Sherman contacted him. Scott had heard good things about Sherman and was anxious to meet this diligent young lieutenant. He invited Sherman to dinner. During the meal, eager to hear the latest news, General Scott quizzed Sherman about the situation in California.

General Scott then sent Sherman to Washington to make a full report to the president and the secretary of war, George W. Crawford. Sherman spent more than an hour briefing President

Taylor on the happenings in California. While in the capital, he also established good relations with George Gibson, the commissary general of subsistence, and with Adjutant General Roger Jones. Sherman's friends began to tease him about being the favorite lieutenant in Washington.

Using this edge, Sherman decided to apply for a position as captain. He hoped to get into the Commissary Department with a recommendation from General Gibson. Sherman saw a shift from line duty to staff duty as a sound career move. He believed that there would be decades of peace ahead. In the peacetime army, he believed, a first lieutenant in the artillery had little chance to win glory or promotion. This would be especially true if most military encounters involved nothing more than skirmishes with American Indians. To Sherman, it seemed as if the rank of captain in the Commissary Department might be the best he could expect. In any case, it would offer enough pay to support a family.

In Washington, Sherman finally was reunited with his bride-to-be. Ellen Ewing now was 26 years old. Her father (and Sherman's adoptive father), Thomas Ewing, now was the secretary of the interior. He lived with his family in the Blair House, a spacious, four-story mansion on Pennsylvania Avenue, near the White House. On an afternoon in mid-February, Ellen was standing in the Blair House conservatory, giving her canary a bath, when she heard footsteps approaching the door. When she turned around, she saw Sherman. It was their first meeting in four years. "Let's get married on May first," said Sherman, who thought that Ellen was even lovelier than he remembered, "and then we can write our day of joy with all nature."

Ellen made wedding plans, and Sherman, now on a six-month leave, mapped out the honeymoon trip. The grand wedding took place at the Blair House in the presence of 300 guests. Among them were President Zachary Taylor and his cabinet as well as a number of congressmen. Sherman said his vows dressed

During his time as secretary of the interior, Thomas Ewing occupied the Blair House, a grand home that was bigger than the White House. Originally built by newspaper publisher Francis Preston Blair in 1824, the Blair House was the setting for the wedding of Ellen Ewing and Sherman.

in full uniform, complete with saber and spurs. The honeymoon took them to Baltimore, Philadelphia, and New York, with stops at Niagara Falls and West Point. The newlyweds then made a short trip to Lancaster, Ohio. After the honeymoon, Ellen and William Sherman spent the summer in Washington, D.C.

Sherman continued to be a familiar face at governmental events. When President Taylor died suddenly in July, Sherman took part in the funeral procession. He was a regular spectator at the great congressional debates that swirled around the Compromise of 1850 and witnessed the heated clashes between Northerners and Southerners in the Senate. When Vice President Millard Fillmore ascended to the presidency, he made some changes. Thomas Ewing lost his cabinet post, but

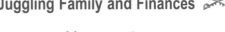

the governor of Ohio promptly appointed him to a Senate seat. The appointment meant that the Ewing family would be moving back to Lancaster.

For the time being, Sherman went along with the Ewings to Ohio. He still firmly believed, however, that he soon would receive one of four new captaincies opening in the Subsistence Department. In September 1850, he finally got the position. He was thrilled to find out that he was to be stationed in St. Louis, Missouri, the department's headquarters. He had always been impressed by the city's clean and prosperous look. In St. Louis, Sherman's official duties were the handling and distribution of foodstuffs and the keeping of accounts related to these supply items. Because Ellen was pregnant, she did not accompany her husband when he left for St. Louis. Neither Ellen Sherman nor her parents felt that she should leave Lancaster until after the baby was born. Sherman reluctantly agreed.

Sherman's role as commissary did not demand much of his time. Without Ellen to keep him company, he immersed himself in a new kind of work. He became an agent and adviser to Thomas Ewing, who owned land around St. Louis and in the wider surrounding area. Sherman collected rent, paid taxes, and bought and sold land for Ewing. He quickly became a talented real estate businessman. Before long, he was making recommendations about the prices Ewing should ask and advising him to sell whenever he was offered a fair price, in case times changed for the worse.

On January 28, 1851, Sherman received a telegram. Ellen had given birth to a daughter, Maria, whom they called Minnie. In March, he traveled to Lancaster to escort his wife and daughter to St. Louis. The family settled into a small house on Chouteau Avenue. Ellen had a hard time adjusting to life so far away from her family, and she desperately missed her hometown of Lancaster.

Ellen was not the only one who was having trouble adjusting. A family was more expensive than Sherman had anticipated. Although he had brought a hefty sum of money back from Monterey, he also had a tendency to hand out loans to family and friends. He had difficulty collecting these debts. Sherman was forced to dip into his savings just to pay monthly bills. "My household expenses here are beyond my means," he wrote to his brother John. "I thought that gradually I might economize, but 'tis impossible." Eventually, Sherman had to send Ellen and Minnie back to Lancaster, although Ellen was pregnant again. During the summer of 1851, Sherman lived with friends in St. Louis.

In 1852, he received orders to report to New Orleans. Sherman was to take the place of Major Waggaman, the current officer in charge of the commissary. In September, just before he left St. Louis, Sherman learned that his mother, Mary, had died suddenly. Overcome with grief, Sherman wrote to Ellen, "Poor Mother! She has had hard times." Still, he did not return to Ohio for her funeral.

Before long, Sherman had the operations in New Orleans completely overhauled. He shopped along the levee for the best quality and the lowest prices. He leased a warehouse and hired a guard, so that he could buy nonperishable items when the prices were low and store them for later use. Although Waggaman had let an outside firm called Perry Seawell and Company do the packing, Sherman had his own people do this work. From time to time, Sherman even rolled up a sleeve and dug down into a barrel of salt pork to make sure the meat was all of good quality. Captain Sherman became well known on the levee, in both commercial and social circles. After all, he was one of the city's major foodstuff purchasers; he bought up sugar, coffee, and ham tons at a time.

Sherman had moved alone to New Orleans to get things settled, but he planned to have Ellen join him as soon as the baby was born. Out of the two years of their marriage, they had been separated from each other half the time. Sherman was tired of being away from his wife and child. In a letter to

Thomas Ewing, he said, "As to [Ellen] being home next summer when you get there I doubt it exceedingly. I think she has been at Lancaster too much since our marriage, and it is time for her to be weaned." Anticipating his family's arrival, Sherman rented a house on Magazine Street. He mailed Ellen a detailed description of the house with a sketch of the floor plan.

In November 1852, in Lancaster, Ellen gave birth to a second daughter, Mary Elizabeth, named after her grandmother. The family called her Lizzie. In late December, Ellen, the two children, a nurse, and Sherman's younger sister Frances arrived in New Orleans. Expenses immediately skyrocketed. Sherman's army pay was adequate to support a family in most places, but it did not cover the cost of living in New Orleans. Moreover, there was nothing his superiors could do to help. His pay was fixed by law.

At about this time, Sherman received a letter from Henry Turner, an old friend who lived in St. Louis. Turner wrote of his plans to undertake a business venture in California. He intended to open a bank in San Francisco—a branch of Lucas, Simonds, and Company of St. Louis, where he was a partner. Having heard about Sherman's tight financial circumstances, he asked the captain to consider joining the venture. Turner promised Sherman a partnership plus a salary. He figured that Sherman's business skills would come in handy. Ever since he left California, Sherman had longed to return. In a letter to Hugh Ewing, as quoted in Michael Fellman's *Citizen Sherman*, Sherman wrote, "My fancy [imagination] will rove [wander] back to Monterey . . . and the wild scenes of Gold Mountain." His California daydreams were enough to strip New Orleans of all its interest and charm.

By the end of February 1853, Sherman had made a deal with Turner. He agreed to manage the bank, on a trial basis, for an annual salary of $5,000 and a one-eighth partnership. He also promised to stay with the bank until January 1, 1860. For the time being, he did not quit the army. Instead, he took a six-month leave to pursue his venture. He sent Ellen and the children back to Lancaster, where they could stay until he set up a home in California. That same day, he auctioned off all of their household goods. On March 6, 1853, he set sail from New Orleans to Nicaragua. There, he crossed to the Pacific by small boat and mule. He then boarded another ship bound for San Francisco, ready to roll the dice on the chance of a grand new fortune.

A WHOLE NEW CALIFORNIA

If Sherman had looked on his voyage to California as a sign of things to come, he probably would have turned right around and headed back to New Orleans. Off the coast of California, his ship struck a reef, and he had to be ferried to shore in a small boat. From that point, he hitched a ride to San Francisco on a schooner loaded with lumber. As the boat entered San Francisco Bay, it was caught by the wind and tipped onto its side. A passing vessel rescued the schooner's men from the water and took them to shore. The sea trip was an unfavorable start to Sherman's adventure, but he refused to let it shake his determination.

San Francisco had grown tremendously since Sherman had been there last. It now boasted a population of 50,000 people. Large brick and granite houses lined newly paved streets. Tall buildings had replaced most of the crude shacks of the early Gold Rush days, and wharves stretched a mile out into the bay. Now, in a single day, sailing ships and steamers brought in as much freight as would have taken an entire month to unload in 1848. In 1850, the value of California gold production had hit $80 million—twice the size of that year's federal budget. This gold flowed into the California economy, bringing with it a rapid boom in wealth and much growth. "This is the most extraordinary place," Sherman exclaimed.

As soon as Sherman stepped ashore, Henry Turner was there to give him a hearty welcome. The new firm of Lucas, Turner, and Company already had rented a room for Sherman

After the discovery of gold in California, the local economy grew exponentially as men from all over the world continued to arrive in San Francisco, hoping to strike it rich. Sherman, who had no interest in becoming a prospector, returned to California to establish a bank that would profit from the region's prosperity. *Above*, businesses and shops on Market Street in San Francisco during the Gold Rush era.

on Montgomery Street. There, Turner briefed Sherman on their financial position. In the California banking business, there was stiff competition. Although business still relied heavily on mining, shipping, lumber, and agriculture also continued to thrive and grow. In addition to exchanging miners' gold and silver for money, the bank would have to provide loans on bonds and mortgages. After reviewing the situation, Sherman insisted that he needed $300,000 worth of capital from the parent company, instead of the $100,000 for which he originally had planned, to operate a successful bank. With this amount, Sherman claimed, the bank easily could earn $100,000 in its first year and repay a portion of the capital to Lucas, Simonds, and Company. Trusting Sherman's advice, Lucas agreed to increase the capital investment.

Sherman soon felt confident about his future. "I know it was experimental and it has resulted even better than was anticipated," he wrote to Thomas Ewing. "I now stand in position as Chief of a Banking House in the Great City on the Pacific." If he still held on to any uncertainties about his bold venture, they quickly dissipated. He knew that he had made the right decision. "There is no doubt that between going to New Orleans as a captain and to California as a banker, there is no comparison," he continued. "There is no doubt of my ability to provide for [my family] handsomely."

In late summer of 1853, Sherman went east to St. Louis to consult with business associates at the home office. He then traveled to Lancaster to pick up Ellen and the children and head back to California. Thomas and Maria Ewing were unable to mask their grief as they watched their daughter and grandchildren prepare to move so far away. The Ewings were an aging couple in a large house, and they were used to the ringing laughter of little children. In an effort to lessen the blow, they begged Ellen to leave two-year-old Minnie with them for a time. Finding it hard to deny Ellen's parents this scrap of comfort, the Shermans agreed. In September 1853, Sherman made his break from the army: He sent in his letter of resignation. Then, with Ellen, Lizzie, and the baby's nurse, he set sail from New York to San Francisco.

The family settled into a rented house on Stockton Street, a narrow dirt road in a decent area of town. At the outset, Ellen detested San Francisco. She was appalled by the city's many dirty streets lined with ramshackle buildings and by the rowdiness of the people, many of whom stayed up all night at gambling saloons. Ellen complained that the house had no backyard, and that the dusty wind whistled through the drafty, unplastered walls. In a letter home, Ellen told her mother, "I am afraid I will never have that happy art that some mothers have of forgetting themselves entirely in their fullness of regard for husband and children." Still, she did her best to make the place homey with their meager possessions.

Trying to ease Ellen's frustration, Sherman bought her a piano. Soon, on most evenings, melodies drifted down the street as Ellen plunked out tunes from memory. The piano was not enough to erase Ellen's longing for Lancaster, however. Then, in February 1854, Sherman bought one side of a brick duplex on Garden Street, with a gorgeous view of the bay. The new house had a parlor, a dining room, and a kitchen on the first floor and four bedrooms on the second floor. It also had a nice backyard in which Lizzie could play.

The new house lifted Ellen's mood. She immediately bought a new table and chairs and a new rug. Sherman began to entertain important San Francisco businessmen and old army buddies at intimate supper parties. With his increasing wealth, Sherman was living in splendid style, and he quickly became one of the most popular and influential men in San Francisco. Eventually, however, Ellen fell back into homesickness. She dwelled on every memory of Ohio. "I would rather live in Lancaster poor than to be a millionaire away from it," she wrote to her mother. "What I wouldn't give to stand one hour in the dear old home with all about me well and happy."

Meanwhile, Sherman buried himself in banking. In his spare time, he sketched out plans for a new building. He supervised affairs at the bank as closely as he had supervised matters as captain of the army commissary. He personally signed all the bills of exchange and insisted on being consulted on loans and discounts. "In banking—as in the army—there can be but one master," he wrote to Hugh Ewing, "and so long as I am here I must occupy that post."

By the end of 1854, Sherman and other businessmen began to detect signs that the economic pulse of the city was slowing. Stock companies were failing, and merchants were struggling with sagging sales. People began to panic. On February 17, 1855, a bank called Page, Bacon, and Company went under. Six days later, Lucas, Turner, and Company felt the aftershock. Tellers at the bank paid off hordes of accounts all day. As the tellers counted out bills with nervous fingers, Sherman displayed coolness, courage, and boldness to improvise—the same coolness under fire for which he became so famous years later. He visited the homes and businesses of his big depositors to reassure them and to borrow extra cash to cover the withdrawals. By three in the afternoon, however, the tellers' money trays were looking slim. Sherman hoped that the bank could hold out until closing time, an hour later. Finally, the clock struck four, and Sherman closed the bank's doors. The bank had survived the run. That night, Sherman made the rounds again to collect more money. He braced himself for another day of heavy withdrawals. The following day was quiet, however, and the bank was saved.

While in San Francisco, Ellen gave birth to two more children. On June 8, 1854, William T. Sherman Jr. was born. Although Sherman had shown little interest in his daughters in their early years, he showered little Willy with affection. Willy had flaming red hair like his father. Another son—Thomas Ewing Sherman—was born on October 12, 1856.

As Sherman closed the bank's books for 1856, he realized that it had been a bad year, not only for Lucas, Turner, and Company, but also for the rest of San Francisco. Things continued to slow down. Eventually, the year of 1857 turned out to be the lowest year of gold production since the initial discovery at Sutter's Mill in 1848. In January 1857, Turner told Sherman that Mr. Lucas of Lucas, Simonds, and Company had decided to close the San Francisco bank. At the same time, Sherman was being offered a position as manager of a new branch to be opened in New York City. Sherman was torn. To leave San Francisco seemed like a personal retreat, a surrender to failure. Also, he adored California and found it hard to say good-bye. Sherman could see signs of economic depression throughout San Francisco, however. He decided that he must leave.

Sherman arranged an early and orderly closing for the bank, but he had to handle the situation delicately. If word of the closing were to get out too soon, it could spark a run. At this point, the bank would not be able to handle it. Sherman began to accumulate cash. He called in as many debts as possible and turned down all new loan applications. By April, he was ready to settle with depositors. He printed a formal closing notice in the newspaper. Luckily, there was no great rush for withdrawals. Some accounts still had money in them even after the April 20 deadline. Two problems remained, however: delinquent accounts and real estate held by the bank. Some debtors simply did not have the money to pay up their accounts, and the current real estate market was too slow to sell all the property owned by the bank. These tied-up assets totaled nearly $300,000. For now, however, there was little Sherman could do.

In May, the Shermans set sail for New York. Ellen was delighted. She and the children were to stay in Lancaster while Sherman gave the job in New York a try. During the trip back East, onboard the steamer *Central America*, the family celebrated Willie's third birthday. By the end of June, Ellen and the children were back in Ohio, and Sherman was on his way to New York.

On July 21, Sherman opened the bank. The address was 12 Wall Street. It was horrible timing for the opening of a new bank. The year saw a steep downturn in the nation's economy that became known as the panic of 1857. This economic crash was caused by a number of factors, including shifts in America's foreign trade arena, rampant land speculation, and, most importantly, the fragility of the country's financial institutions. The

In 1857, the Ohio Life Insurance and Trust Company collapsed, causing fear and worry to overwhelm the financial world. Frantic, people began withdrawing their money from banks, causing even more bankruptcies and further exacerbating the crisis. Known as the Panic of 1857 *(depicted in the painting above)*, the financial downturn forced Sherman to return home without a job as his bank folded.

number of banks in the United States had doubled in the past decade. There were 60 banks in New York alone. At that time, there were no federal regulations on banks and no insurance on accounts. Some banks did not have enough money on hand to back up what they had loaned out.

The first bank to fail was the New York branch of the Ohio Life Insurance and Trust Company; it crumbled four days after Sherman opened for business. The collapse took down two dozen other banks in New York and choked out the New York bank's parent firm in Cincinnati. Many New York bankers were counting on a fresh transfusion of money from California to help them survive. This money, in the form of gold from the San Francisco Mint, was to arrive in New York on the *Central America*, the same ship on which the Shermans had celebrated Willy's birthday in June. On September 12, news broke that the ship had gone down in a hurricane off the Carolina coast, taking with it to the ocean floor more than 400 passengers and several tons of gold.

The nation panicked. Two weeks later, the Bank of Pennsylvania folded. Then, on the morning of October 7, Sherman awoke to find out that Lucas, Simonds, and Company of St. Louis had closed the New York branch. Sherman walked to Wall Street, filled up a trunk with as many of the bank's assets as he could pack, and boarded a train to St. Louis. He stayed there for the rest of the year to sort out what was left of the Lucas empire. He also made one more trip to California to try to collect as many debts as he could.

By July 1858, Sherman had done all that he could. Now almost penniless, he headed back East. All of the time and effort he had invested in the banking venture seemed lost. On the voyage, he wrote to a friend, "I go to Lancaster, Ohio to start where I began 22 years ago." Unlike his wife, William Tecumseh Sherman did not want to live permanently in Lancaster. There, he would always be Cump Sherman. He wanted more from life.

BLEEDING KANSAS

Ellen's brother Tom practiced law in Leavenworth, Kansas. With the passage of the Kansas-Nebraska Act in 1854, the ban against slavery in the Western territories had been lifted. The North (antislavery) and the South (proslavery) both were determined to have Kansas enter the Union on their side. No one, it seems, wanted to let the territory alone to work out its own destiny. Kansas became a testing ground—and, later, a battlefield. In November 1854, an election was held in Kansas to choose a delegate to Congress. A large group of Missourians crossed over into the territory to insure the election of a pro-slavery congressman. In March 1855, about 5,000 people from Missouri again crossed the border, this time to vote for a slave code and strict laws against abolitionist actions. Kansas settlers who were against slavery refused to recognize this legislation. They held their own elections. By January 1856, there were two governments in Kansas—one built on fraud and the other created outside the law.

President Franklin Pierce denounced the Free State (antislavery) government and encouraged proslavery Kansans to take action. In May, proslavery ruffians attacked the antislavery town of Lawrence. This action inspired abolitionist John Brown to strike back. He and a band of men swooped down on a proslavery settlement on Pottawatomie Creek. Brown's gang dragged five settlers out of their cabins and murdered them. The slaughter, called the Pottawatomie Massacre, sparked a small-scale war between proslavery and antislavery settlers that later became known as Bleeding Kansas. By the end of 1856, about 200 people in Kansas had been killed in these skirmishes.

Sherman's brother John had been elected to Congress in 1854. Vehemently opposed to slavery, John Sherman believed that the new Western territories should be kept free. He strongly supported the Missouri Compromise of 1820, which stopped the expansion of slavery into new Western territories. In 1818, Missouri had applied for statehood as a slave state. If the application had been accepted, slave states would have held a majority of seats in the U.S. Senate. At that time, New York congressional representative James Tallmadge introduced an amendment to the admission bill that prohibited any further spread of slavery in Missouri. Furthermore, the amendment said, any slave born in Missouri would be emancipated, or freed, at age 25. The amended admission bill easily passed the House of Representatives, but it died in the proslavery-majority Senate, where it never came up for a vote.

Then, in 1819, the free territory of Maine applied for statehood. Speaker of the House Henry Clay saw an opportunity to keep a balance of free and slave states in the Senate. He made a proposal. In it, Maine and Missouri would have to be admitted together—one as a free state and one as a slave state. Clay persuaded Northern congressmen to drop the amendment that forbade slavery in Missouri. At the same time, Clay won the approval of Southern congressmen to a proposal that slavery be limited to lands below 36°30' north latitude, the southern border of Missouri, in the rest of the Western territories. This agreement left the unsettled portion of the Louisiana Purchase that lay north and west of Missouri free from slavery. The only territories in which slavery could spread were in the area of present-day Arkansas and Oklahoma. The proposal, known as the Missouri Compromise, was passed. It postponed the impending conflict, at least for a time.

THE MISSOURI COMPROMISE OF 1850

The Compromise of 1850, which admitted California as a free state, reopened the issue of how to handle new territories. Under this compromise, the rest of the land acquired in the Mexican War—Utah and New Mexico, and parts of Nevada, Colorado, and Arizona—could be admitted without any mention of slavery. Each new state could decide for itself whether it wanted to be slave or free. As it turned out, both Utah and New Mexico were admitted as slave states.

Slavery was not the only issue dividing North and South at this time. The regions differed strongly on the matter of states' rights. In the South, the states wanted the right to make their own laws, including laws on slavery. In the North, people favored a strong federal government that had a hand in making laws for all the states. The Compromise of 1850 was an attempt to keep Southern states from leaving the Union.

In 1850, as part of the compromise, Congress also passed a Fugitive Slave Act. This law proved to be highly controversial. At times, slaves who escaped from their owners in the South fled to free Northern states. These slaves often used the Underground Railroad—a system of safe houses through which abolitionists helped runaway slaves escape to freedom. Slaveholders wanted to make sure that anyone who helped runaway slaves was punished. The Fugitive Slave Act of 1850 stated that all escaped slaves must be returned to their owners. If any person failed to turn in an escaped slave, he or she could be slapped with a hefty fine, imprisoned, or both.

Many Northerners chose to ignore this law. In fact, many Northern states passed their own laws that made the Fugitive Slave Act basically null and void. Refusal of Northern states to enforce the Fugitive Slave Act was one of the reasons that led South Carolina to secede from the Union in 1860.

In 1854, the Kansas-Nebraska Act overturned the Missouri Compromise. This added to an already intense debate. Instead of states above 36°30' north latitude being admitted as free states, the Kansas-Nebraska Act allowed the territories to decide for themselves whether they wanted to be slave or free states. It was at this point that the violence of Bleeding Kansas broke out.

In Washington, D.C., Sherman's brother, Representative John Sherman, defended the Kansas antislavery movement and criticized President Pierce for his proslavery comments. Although John Sherman opposed the expansion of slavery, he was against government interference in existing slave states. John Sherman did not want to see slavery spread, but he did not think that it should be abolished in every state. Many Northern politicians shared this view. Their main objective was to keep

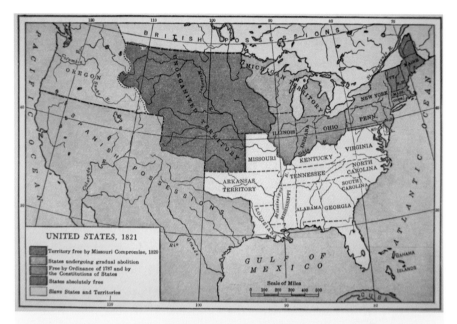

UNITED STATES, 1821

Territory free by Missouri Compromise, 1820
States undergoing gradual abolition
Free by Ordinance of 1787 and by the Constitutions of States
States absolutely free
Slave States and Territories

After the Panic of 1857, shades of the upcoming civil war began to creep into everyday life as the continued bickering between the North and South divided the nation over slavery. Like his brother, Sherman did not oppose slavery but believed in preserving the Union. As people throughout the country argued about the status of new states and territories, Sherman debated on his future and considered rejoining the military. *Above*, a map of the United States in the 1850s shows the free states, slave states, and different territories in North America at the time.

the Union from splitting apart. The only way to accomplish this goal was to allow slavery in the Southern states. William T. Sherman agreed with his brother on this matter. "The [blacks] of our country should remain slaves," he said in a letter to John. "I would prefer to have them subject [under the control of another], than in any other political position, where in numbers they approach in equality the whites."

While all this was going on, Tom Ewing offered Sherman a position as a partner in his firm in Leavenworth, Kansas. The job involved keeping the books and handling collections. Sherman accepted it. If things worked out, Ellen and the children could follow later. Leavenworth was an army town. In fact, it was not much more than a fort. Sherman quickly made many army friends. He easily passed the Kansas bar; the judge admitted him on "general knowledge." Still, Sherman felt like an imposter as a lawyer. He dreaded the day that he would have to defend a client in court. When that time finally came, he floundered and lost the case. He based his argument on a law that had been repealed 30 years earlier.

In early November 1858, Ellen arrived in Leavenworth with three of the children. Minnie, who had grown attached to her grandparents, stayed behind. Sherman did not last long in Leavenworth, however. In San Francisco, he had made an annual salary of $5,000. After six months in Leavenworth, he had earned only $650. In March 1859, Ellen, pregnant again, returned to Lancaster with the children. That year, Sherman moved to Indian Springs, Kansas, to homestead for Thomas Ewing. One of the Ewing relatives wanted a farm prepared there. To get the place ready for the family to move in, Sherman built a barn, a few sheds, and a corncrib. He also planted some fruit trees. During these months on the prairie, Sherman reflected on his life. He had given up on the one career he was trained to do and had failed in the civilian world. Now nearly 40 years old, he found himself toiling at sweaty, grueling farmwork.

Sherman then heard, through the army grapevine, that there were personnel problems in the Paymaster's Department, the only army department in which a civilian could be hired. Perhaps this could be his way back into the army. At once, Sherman wrote to Don Carlos Buell, an old army comrade who had graduated from West Point one year behind Sherman. Now, Buell was a high-ranking officer in the War Department. Buell wrote back with unfortunate news: Any vacancy in the Paymaster's Department would likely be filled by someone from the South. Buell knew of another job opening, however. Officials in the state of Louisiana were setting up a school that would be organized and run by the military. The school's board of supervisors was looking for a superintendent for the new Louisiana State Seminary of Learning and Military Academy, and Buell would gladly recommend Sherman. The school still exists: It is known today as Louisiana State University (LSU).

As soon as Sherman got the news, he wrote a four-page letter of application to Louisiana governor R.B. Wickliffe. A series of lucky circumstances helped open the door for Sherman. For starters, because Buell had received advance notice of the position (he knew the president of the new school), Sherman got a jump on other applicants. Also, George Mason Graham was on the school's board of supervisors. Not only had Buell served with Graham in the Mexican War, he also had married the widow of Graham's half brother, Richard B. Mason—Sherman's commanding officer in California. Graham's sister taught at the Academy of the Visitation (also known as Visitation Academy), where Ellen Ewing had been one of her favorite pupils. One board member objected violently, however. He pointed out that Sherman was "the son-in-law of that black-hearted abolitionist Tom Ewing." Despite the opposition, Graham managed to get Sherman elected to the post. As the new superintendent and professor of engineering, Sherman received a $3,500 annual salary.

LOUISIANA

In October 1859, Sherman left for Alexandria, Louisiana, hoping that his fortunes now were about to improve. If things did not go well, he figured that he could find work back in Ohio at the Hocking Valley salt wells. The region around Alexandria was remote and sparsely populated. To reach New Orleans, the nearest city of any substantial size, meant a 35-hour trip by stagecoach and steamboat. There was only one house near the school, a house that Professor Anthony Vallas already had rented. Another house was to be built for Sherman. Ellen and the children were to join Sherman in Alexandria as soon as the house was finished. The Sherman children now numbered five: little Eleanor Mary, called

"Elly," had been born in September. The delay in bringing the family probably was for the best. The wilderness of Louisiana was no place for Ellen and the children: There were no shops,

THE ABOLITION MOVEMENT

Often called the antislavery movement, the abolition movement sought to end the enslavement of Africans and people of African descent in Europe, the Americas, and Africa itself. Abolitionists also worked to end the Atlantic slave trade between Africa, Europe, and the Americas.

Slavery began in the area of North America that later became the United States in 1619, when a Dutch soldier brought 20 Africans to the English colony of Jamestown, Virginia, and sold them as indentured servants. Indentured servants agreed to work without pay for a certain number of years, after which they were free.

African Americans were not the only indentured servants in the colonies, however. In the early 1600s, some Europeans who wanted to sail to America could not afford to pay for their passage. Plantation owners paid the travel expenses for these immigrants if they agreed to become indentured servants. At that time, anyone who bought passage to Virginia received 50 acres of land. By buying passage for indentured servants, plantation owners enlarged their farms and gained workers at the same time.

By the late 1600s, there was a shortage of indentured servants coming to the colonies. Plantation owners still needed workers to tend their vast crops, however. In 1690, slave traders began to bring Africans to the colonies. Eventually, the traders were bringing up to 10,000 slaves each year. Most of these Africans were kidnapped. They were bound in chains and forced to leave their homelands and families forever.

no doctors, and no Catholic church. Awaiting the building of his house, Sherman took a room at a tavern four miles from the school.

By the early 1800s, wealthy landowners had built large plantations throughout the Southern United States. There, the warm climate allowed planters to grow many crops. Until the Civil War, plantations were the most important businesses in the South. The number of black slaves in the South grew from 650,000 in 1790 to nearly 4 million by 1861. Slave traders stopped bringing enslaved people from West Africa to the United States in 1808. Plantation owners continued to buy and sell American-born black slaves, however.

By the late 1700s, many people in the United States, especially in the North, opposed slavery. Many Northerners wanted to end slavery in all the states, and the abolitionist movement grew. By 1804, slavery had been abolished in most Northern states. It remained legal along the border with the South, in Delaware, Kentucky, Maryland, and Missouri. Because these states remained loyal to the Union at the time of the Civil War, they remained slave states even after the Emancipation Proclamation freed the slaves in the rebellious states in 1863.

Abolitionists hid runaway slaves from slave catchers and helped slaves escape to the North on the Underground Railroad. This system of safe houses and secret routes ran from Southern states to the Northern states and Canada. The Fugitive Slave Act of 1850 made it illegal for anyone to hide slaves or help them to escape. Many abolitionists continued to operate the Underground Railroad despite the law, however, and allowed thousands of slaves to escape to freedom.

The Louisiana State Seminary of Learning and Military Academy was scheduled to open in January 1860. With much preparation still to be done, the academy needed a superintendent with initiative, energy, and diligence. Sherman fit the bill. Borrowing heavily from the rulebook of the Virginia Military Institute, Sherman, Graham, and several other board members outlined school regulations. Today, the original draft, written by Sherman, is preserved in the LSU library.

Even as Sherman was preoccupied with preparations for opening the academy, other events in the South were electrifying the nation and hastening what looked to be an inevitable clash between North and South. John Brown, the leader of the 1856 Pottawatomie Massacre, hatched a plot to liberate slaves and, with them, found a new nation in the mountains of western Virginia—a nation of which Brown would be the commander in chief. The first step in his scheme was to attack the federal arsenal at Harpers Ferry, Virginia, in what is now West Virginia. Brown planned to distribute the arms he would capture there to local slaves, thereby instigating a rebellion.

On the night of October 16, 1859, Brown and a posse of 21 men, including four of his sons, launched an assault on the arsenal. Because the arsenal was defended by a single guard, this capture was not difficult. During the attack, only one man in Brown's group was killed—an unarmed free African-American railroad worker. Next, Brown took 60 prominent local citizens hostage; one of the hostages was a descendant of George Washington. Brown then cut telegraph wires and blocked railroad tracks in an attempt to keep military reinforcements away from Harpers Ferry. Originally, Brown hoped to rally 500 slaves to join his army. Only 10 slaves fled their owners to join Brown's rebellion, however.

Within hours of the attack, local militia and every townsman with a weapon showed up at Harpers Ferry. During the ensuing fight, Brown and some of his followers were forced to take refuge in a small brick firehouse. Two members of Brown's gang were killed and used as target practice by the enraged townsmen. Word of Brown's raid was sent to Washington by telegraph. The next day, a small force of Marines, led by army lieutenant Robert E. Lee, was hastily dispatched to Harpers Ferry. When Brown refused to surrender, the Marines launched a swift assault. Within three minutes, all of Brown's men were either killed or captured. Ten of the raiders were killed or mortally wounded, including two of Brown's sons. Seven were taken prisoner, including John Brown. Five managed to escape. Brown's men killed five Marines and wounded nine others. On October 31, Brown was convicted of treason, conspiring with slaves to commit treason, and murder. He was hanged on December 2, 1859.

Undoubtedly, Sherman knew of John Brown's raid and its aftermath. Because he was against the abolitionist movement, Sherman probably felt that justice had been served on John Brown. Sherman was too busy with the seminary, however, to give the situation in Harpers Ferry too much attention. The new academy could accommodate up to 160 cadets. In that first year, Sherman expected it to be filled to capacity. As the first day of classes drew nearer, however, it looked as if just 59 cadets would attend. On January 2, only 18 of the 59 reported to school. Others trickled in as the semester got under way. Because the new school had a limited faculty, Sherman taught architecture and drawing.

Just as Sherman was getting accustomed to academic life, another opportunity arose. A group of entrepreneurs, including Hugh Ewing, planned to open a bank in London, England. One of the men showed up in Louisiana to make a dazzling offer to Sherman. A two-year contract with the London bank would pay Sherman $7,500 a year—more than twice what he was making at the seminary. Ellen and the other Ewings naturally thought that this was too good an opportunity to pass up. After some negotiation, however, Sherman decided to stay at the seminary.

Sherman tried to convince Ellen that she could have a peaceful life in Louisiana. As 1859 ended and 1860 began, however, Louisiana was anything but tranquil. In the wake of John Brown's raid and other abolitionist outbursts, some board members at the seminary began to question Sherman's loyalty to the South. He was, after all, a Northerner. On hearing these accusations, Sherman plainly stated that he was not opposed to slavery. At the same time, he held a solid and unwavering opposition to secession.

The school faced problems. At West Point, most cadets were there on four-year scholarships—grants that both the cadets and their parents considered too valuable to risk. At the Louisiana seminary, parents paid for their sons' education. If the workload began to seem too heavy for the young men, what would keep the parents from pulling their sons out and sending them to some other school? Sherman's solution was to make the program less difficult and more pleasing to the cadets. He believed that the strict, military-style rule of West Point would only scare cadets away.

In truth, many parents probably thought that military discipline was just what their sons needed. The cadets had much leisure time, and most of them were not well behaved. The academy had enrolled its fair share of spoiled, headstrong young men who were used to getting their own way and ordering servants around. The parents of the cadets handed their responsibility over to Sherman, who was not quite sure how to deal with such men. Without any clear rules for Sherman to follow, his disciplinary practices varied from case to case. Some of his punishments sparked controversy.

In January 1860, a heated argument between two cadets named Hyams and Haworth turned into a brawl. Fuming, Haworth stormed to his room. He snatched up his Bowie knife and went prowling for Hyams. Before Haworth could carry out his plan, Sherman caught him. He expelled the hot-tempered cadet on the spot. Later, when Sherman learned that Hyams had started the fight, he expelled Hyams as well. Soon afterward, Hyams's father showed up at the seminary with a judge, ready to contest Sherman's decision.

In June, a series of nasty pranks broke out, perpetrated by a nighttime gang called the Midnight Marauders. Sherman tackled the cases in the manner of a private detective. The gang's activities carried ridiculous names, such as "The Mose Chicken Case," "The Bucket Case," and "The Affair at the Spring." In the last-named incident, the group tossed a slave into a stream.

Sherman uncovered two leaders of the gang: cadets named Campbell and Ringgold. The two admitted their roles in the mischief, but the confessions were not enough for Sherman. He wanted other cadets who were eyewitnesses to testify against their classmates. The other cadets refused to talk, however. Sherman tried to reason with them. He explained that they should not conceal wrongs just because they did not want to be considered tattletales. Two cadets—Stafford and Hillen—quit the academy rather than implicate their friends. The captain of the Marauders, a cadet named Liddell, also quit in protest. Furious with the cadets, Sherman insisted that Liddell's unauthorized departure be listed as desertion, even as the cadet's father vehemently disputed the designation.

Some board members also thought that Sherman's punishments were too severe. The board as a whole must not have been too concerned, however. Not wanting to lose Sherman to the London banking venture, they offered him a $500–per-year raise to stay. For the most part, Sherman managed to run the seminary efficiently. There was never a class called off or a drill canceled. Sherman even organized a social life for the cadets. He planned periodic dances, called hops, and invited the daughters of local planters. He also held an elaborate ball at which the cadets could show off their dress uniforms.

As the days of 1860 ticked by, the national crisis grew more grave. During the summer, the upcoming presidential election dominated conversation. Even the cadets seemed nervous. All eyes were fixed on South Carolina, which had threatened to secede from the Union if Abraham Lincoln won the election. In November, Lincoln was elected president. In December, South Carolina made good on its threat and withdrew from the Union. It was followed quickly by six other states—Mississippi, Florida, Alabama, Georgia, Texas, and Louisiana.

Sherman foresaw the coming destruction of the entire country. His strong views on secession forced him to leave Louisiana and head back to Ohio. Because the seminary still owed him $500 of his salary, however, he stayed in Alexandria until February 19. He then traveled to New Orleans, where he stayed a day or two before moving on to Lancaster to be reunited with his family. He left the Deep South far behind him. The next time he returned, it was with an army.

Back in Uniform

Both the North and the South believed that the conflict would be a short one. Sherman, however, predicted a long struggle. In the spring of 1861, he said that the war would last 30 years. At other times, he suggested that it would rage on for half a century. In 1864, just six months before the Confederates surrendered at Appomattox, he spoke again of 30 more years of fighting. Sherman did not view the conflict in terms of slavery, states' rights, cruelty, or bankruptcy. In his mind, these issues were minor. For him, the war pivoted on the breaking of the Union. Secession was the final, fateful challenge to a government that Sherman saw as nearly perfect.

In February 1861, Sherman tentatively accepted a position in St. Louis as president of the Fifth Street Railway, a streetcar line. Before he took up his new post, his brother

John—who thought Sherman should rejoin the army—took him to Washington to meet the new president. They reached the capital on March 6 and went straight to the White House. President Lincoln had been in office for only 48 hours, and the city was swarming with people. The two brothers cut their way through the crowds to reach the president.

John Sherman tried to get Lincoln's attention. "Mr. President, this is my brother, Colonel Sherman, who is just up from Louisiana," he said. "He may give you some information you want."

Not looking too worried about the current situation in the South, Lincoln turned to William T. Sherman. "Ah! How are they getting along down there?" he asked.

"They think they are getting along swimmingly," replied Sherman. "They are preparing for war."

"Oh, well!" Lincoln said. "I guess we'll manage to keep house." Lincoln then brushed Sherman off, claiming that he had no need for military men at this point.

Sherman was offended by the boisterous atmosphere at the White House and by the casual attitude of President Lincoln. The new administration seemed to be clueless about the catastrophe that Sherman felt lay ahead. Lincoln and his advisers, Sherman believed, were sleeping on a volcano.

Sherman was less than eager to rejoin the army. A few months earlier, he would have jumped at the chance to get back into uniform. Now, he stalled. Even as a showdown loomed at Fort Sumter, South Carolina, Sherman failed to answer several calls for his service. He closely followed events as they unfolded in Charleston Harbor that April. The place was of special interest to him, as he had served there. Also, Fort Sumter now was commanded by Robert Anderson. He was a longtime friend who had been Sherman's company commander in Florida 20 years earlier.

Anderson was in desperate need of supplies and reinforcements. South Carolina, in the grip of secession fever, believed

Located in South Carolina, Fort Sumter was a Federal stronghold occupied by Union troops when the state seceded from the Union. Soldiers of the newly formed Confederate States of America demanded that the Federal troops evacuate the fort, which they considered to be Confederate property. The attack on Fort Sumter marked the beginning of armed conflict in the Civil War.

that the harbor fort belonged to the newly formed Southern government, the Confederate States of America, rather than to the Union. On April 12, when Union soldiers tried to hold the fort, Confederate troops opened fire. After three days, the Confederates and the Union called a truce. Although the confrontation was hailed as a victory in the North because the Confederates lowered their flag, Southerners were appalled. Virginia, Arkansas, North Carolina, and Tennessee quickly seceded and joined the Confederacy.

Meanwhile, by the end of March, Sherman and his family had settled in St. Louis. He went to work at the Fifth Street Railway for a salary of $2,000 a year. Soon, he realized that he was in yet another financial bind. With expenses that topped $300 per month, there was no way he could make ends meet.

Sherman had a front-row seat to the struggle over secession in Missouri. Although it was a slave state, and one in which there was much agitation and strife, Missouri decided to side with the Union. After the fall of Fort Sumter, Lincoln called for 75,000 volunteers. Sherman thought that he should have set the number at 300,000. Sherman wrote to his brother John to say that he would consider rejoining the army only in a high-ranking position. He offered some advice that could be delivered to General Winfield Scott, as well. If Scott planned to move against Richmond, the Confederate capital, it would be best to wait until the Confederate Congress was in session. The psychological impact would be greater, Sherman felt, if the city was defeated during this time. Sherman also shared his opinions about the Union's current military leaders. In Sherman's mind, General Irvin McDowell had spent too much of his service in an office chair, and John Wool could not be trusted. Wool had failed Sherman at a critical moment in California, when Sherman needed military support during a riot in San Francisco. Sherman was confident, however, in John McClellan. Sherman considered him the army's best man.

Throughout the Union, men were rushing to arms. The Union Army was desperately seeking anyone with military expertise. John Sherman was becoming impatient with his brother. He insisted that William T. Sherman could take command of the Ohio militia with a rank of major general if he showed even the slightest interest.

Finally, on May 8, Sherman wrote a brief letter to Secretary of War Simon Cameron, offering his services. He explained that he had not volunteered right away because, with his background, he felt unwilling to take a simple soldier's job. As it turned out, Congress had just created several new regiments in the army. Colonel Sherman could take command of one of these regiments. On June 6, 1861, Sherman was summoned to Washington. Once again, Ellen and the children went back to Lancaster, and Sherman dusted off his uniform.

BULL RUN

In Washington, D.C., Sherman became commanding officer of the 13th U.S. Infantry Regiment. At the end of June, he received new orders to take command of a brigade of volunteers that was stationed at Fort Corcoran—one of the forts guarding the U.S. capital. The fort was located on eight acres of a country estate called Rosslyn, which served as the temporary home of several militia regiments. Five of these regiments— the 13th, the 29th, the 69th, and the 79th New York Regiments and the 2nd Wisconsin—belonged to Sherman's brigade. The volunteers were barely infantrymen. They had not much more experience than a passing knowledge of rifles. The men knew nothing at all about the cannon they would be firing in battle. Sherman's brigade of 3,400 officers and men reminded him of the green cadets of the first days at the seminary in Louisiana. He could not help but wonder what would happen if these raw troops had to fight. He soon found out.

Pressures to meet the enemy in battle had been building. Two Confederate armies shadowed northern Virginia and posed a constant menace to the nation's capital. Against his better judgment, General Scott ordered General McDowell to advance, and the orders followed down the line, through the divisions, brigades, and regiments of Sherman's hastily constructed and untried army. Sherman dashed off one last letter to Ellen, unsure of his future in battle. "Whatever befalls me," he wrote, "I know that you appreciate what good qualities I possess . . . and that under your care our children will grow up on the safe side." As recounted in Lee Kennet's *Sherman*, he then concluded, "Goodbye and believe me always most affectionately yours." On the afternoon of July 16, General McDowell put his army in motion.

The long columns of men and vehicles trudged westward along the dusty roads of Virginia. Shepherding the regiments through the Virginia countryside turned out to be quite a challenge for Sherman. A fiery July heat forced the men to make frequent stops to fill their canteens. All along the road, Confederate troops had chopped down trees to block the way, making the march slow and cumbersome. Confusion arose about the order of the march and the route. There were traffic jams caused by cattle herds and supply columns unable to find their destinations. Although the men awoke to reveille at 3:00 A.M., they were not ready to move until almost three hours later. Along the way, men lingered in villages, breaking the column and rejoining it later, armed with a ham or a pail of milk. After two-and-a-half days, the column had moved only 20 miles, to Centreville.

On July 18, the 3rd Brigade had its first encounter with battle. The brief bombardment at Blackburn's Ford lasted just 30 minutes. The brigade was not under Sherman's command, but his soldiers had a good view of the skirmish. Sherman used the engagement to teach his men a little about battle. He told them it was a waste of time to duck when they heard gunfire. By the time they heard the pop of a gun, he noted, the bullet already will have zoomed past. This advice had barely left Sherman's lips when a bullet came whizzing through the trees just a few feet above his head. Immediately, he ducked down, close to his horse's saddle. When he straightened up, he saw a line of smirking faces. "Well, boys," he said, as a smile spread across his face, "you may dodge the big ones."

Once again, the troops pushed forward. This time, they headed toward certain battle. Confederate troops held strong defensive positions facing east and northeast, along the banks of a tributary of the Potomac River known as Bull Run. Confederate general Pierre G.T. Beauregard planned to launch a heavy attack on the Union's left flank. The Union's General McDowell hammered the first strike, however. He attacked the Confederate

The Battle of Bull Run *(above)* was the first major loss for the Union Army and presented a startling reality for many Northerners who thought the war was going to be a short-lived affair. Under the leadership of George McClellan, Union troops were moving south towards Richmond, Virginia, when they were defeated at Bull Run and retreated back toward Washington, D.C.

left flank with his main forces. McDowell then set off on a wide swoop northward as he unleashed another assault at a stone bridge where the Warrenton Turnpike crossed Bull Run. At eight forty-five on the morning of July 21, 1861, the opening shots were fired in the First Battle of Manassas (Bull Run)—a clash that stretched throughout the scorching afternoon.

The Union launched several gallant charges, but the Confederates managed to hold firm. Although outgunned, the Confederates maintained order. Beauregard ordered an all-out charge. Whooping and hollering, the Rebels started off in a stampede. They pierced the Union line at the center, but the thrust was not enough to break it. The battle raged on. By

3:00, it looked as if the Union might win. Beauregard, however, refused to accept defeat. He ordered another charge. This time, the Union soldiers were thrown back. The Union troops fell away from their ranks and dispersed in a chaotic retreat. The Confederate advance came at a high price, however.

When the smoke cleared and the dust settled, a field strewn with mangled bodies came into sharp view. The moans of bleeding soldiers begging for a drink of water floated through the humid air. Over everything there hung the stench of death. Union casualties reached 2,600 to 3,000, including between 460 and 480 men killed. On the Confederate side, there were nearly 2,000 casualties. Of this number, about 375 lay dead. Confederate colonel Thomas "Stonewall" Jackson's brigade suffered the heaviest toll: 119 dead and 442 wounded.

The Union Army marched back to Washington, bedraggled and exhausted. On the retreat, Sherman managed to maintain a degree of control over his men. At one point, he formed them into a defensive position and faced down the pursuing Confederate cavalry. Sherman's men had fought well on Henry House Hill, but they suffered more casualties than other Union brigades. Although no honors were handed out for the lost battle, Sherman's performance was noted by his superiors. He was promoted to brigadier general ahead of other capable commanders including Ambrose Burnside, George H. Thomas, and Ulysses S. Grant.

When the troops were back in Washington, D.C., President Lincoln visited Fort Corcoran to talk with the soldiers and offer his encouragement. At one point in the day, an officer pushed his way through the troops to the president. The officer announced that he had a complaint: Colonel Sherman had threatened to shoot him. Apparently, the officer had wanted to make a trip to New York on business, and Sherman had denied him leave. The confrontation had turned vicious and ended with Sherman shouting that, if the officer tried to leave without permission, he would shoot him "like a dog."

Facing the angry officer, President Lincoln did his best to defuse the situation with a little bit of humor. "Well, if I were you, and he threatened to shoot," the president said, "I would trust him, for I believe he would do it." The soldiers who stood nearby burst out laughing. The officer sheepishly turned around and disappeared into the crowd.

In August, Sherman was called to the White House for a conference with President Lincoln and General Scott. Among those present was Sherman's former company commander Robert Anderson. Anderson asked Sherman to meet him at Willard's Hotel for a discussion about the situation in Kentucky. Having recently taken over the Department of the Cumberland—the Kentucky division of the Union Army— Anderson found himself in a crisis. Kentucky, a border state, was in a precarious situation. Anderson, a Kentucky native, was sent there to keep the state from leaving the Union. Basically, his mission was to offer assistance to pro-Union forces in Kentucky in the hope of maintaining control of the state. He could take with him three brigadier generals of his choosing. He picked Thomas, Burnside, and Sherman. Sherman was to be his second in command.

Anderson and Sherman met with the president several times to discuss the mission. During one conference, Sherman made an unusual request of Lincoln. Sherman wanted the president to assure him that he would serve only as Anderson's second and would not be asked to take command himself. Lincoln gladly granted his request, with a chuckle. He found it refreshing to meet an officer who was not looking for advancement. In truth, Sherman was more worried about leading a losing battle. He did not want to take command of an army until he "saw daylight ahead."

PHANTOM DANGERS IN KENTUCKY

The stakes were high. If Kentucky joined the Confederacy, the South would have the state's ample resources at its disposal and an excellent defensive position along the Ohio River. According to President Lincoln, if the Union lost Kentucky, it would be "nearly the same as to lose the whole game." In May 1861, Kentucky announced that it would remain neutral in the war. Then, that summer, the state held elections, and the majority of representatives elected were pro-Union. Kentucky shifted its position in favor of the Union, but its citizens were concerned about the military consequences of such a decision. It was at this point that Anderson and Sherman stepped in.

On September 1, Sherman stopped in Cincinnati, Ohio, where Ellen, Willie, and Lizzie joined him for a brief visit. Sherman was disappointed that Ellen could not bring along little Rachel—the sixth Sherman, born in July 1860. On September 3, Confederate general Leonidas Polk seized Columbus, Kentucky. Three days later, the Union's General Grant occupied Paducah. Now, both sides had violated Kentucky's neutrality.

Anderson already was in Louisville, Kentucky, setting up headquarters. Sherman visited the governors of the neighboring states of Indiana, Illinois, and Missouri, hoping to secure troops for the coming battles. While Sherman was away, the Kentucky legislature voted to stay in the Union and demanded that Southern forces be removed from the state.

In mid-September, the Confederates had three camps in southern Kentucky. Polk's force was at Columbus. At the other end of the state, a small Rebel army led by General Felix Zollicoffer had taken control of the Cumberland Gap, the only easy passageway through the mountainous region that connected Kentucky with its neighbor to the south—Confederate Tennessee. On September 9, General Simon Bolivar Buckner had occupied Bowling Green. The Confederate hold on southern Kentucky was secured further by two hastily built strongholds: Fort Henry, on the Tennessee River, and Fort Donelson, on the Cumberland River. These three forces were under Confederate commander Albert Sidney Johnston. Like the

Union troops, they were poorly armed and roughly trained, and throughout 1861, their numbers failed to exceed 27,000.

When Sherman reached Louisville, Anderson sent him to set up a protective force around a railroad that ran southwest toward Bowling Green. This railroad was a key link to both Louisville and Nashville, Tennessee. About 30 miles out of Louisville, the railroad crossed streams and gorges over a series of trestles. To protect these, Sherman was supposed to secure a strong defensive position at nearby Muldraugh Hill. As Sherman neared Muldraugh Hill, however, he saw that the spot was not entirely satisfactory as a defensive strongpoint. The Union supply lines were shaky, and the enemy could easily move around the Union troops, burn the trestles, cut the telegraph lines, and isolate the Union forces. Sherman also received the unsettling news that the Confederates were on the move.

Suddenly, Anderson summoned Sherman back to Louisville. Anderson had requested to be relieved of his command and had named Sherman as his successor. The War Department already had approved Anderson's recommendation, and Sherman was to take over as commander of the Army of the Cumberland. Sherman now had much more than Muldraugh Hill to fret about. The fate of Kentucky rested on his shoulders. From the start, Sherman worried that he faced certain failure. He wrote to Ellen, "Tell Willy that I am very anxious to leave him a name of which he will not be ashamed."

Forced to take command against his will—and over a broken promise from President Lincoln—Sherman believed that he needed 300,000 men to reach just half the troop strength that he felt he really needed. His request for this extravagant number was the first of many such calls that Sherman made for more manpower.

Sherman did not inherit a well-organized command. There was a severe shortage of trained personnel, and he lacked competent officers in the field. This was an army of amateurs. Because no one knew the rules or correct procedures and policies, Sherman had to draft and issue all general orders himself. He spent many long afternoons at his desk, filling out a mountain paperwork. He issued duties to the mapmaker and drew up an elaborate set of regulations for the medical unit. In addition, the financial needs of the Department of the Cumberland were barely being met. Caught short financially, Sherman took out a loan just to cover headquarter expenses.

His biggest shortage was in materials—supplies and equipment. General Anderson had put it frankly in a note to Lincoln: "We need everything." The Army of the Cumberland lacked maps of Kentucky, winter clothing, tents, and weapons. Soldiers cleared off the racks at local gun shops. Experienced officers were a rarity. At Bull Run, Sherman had commanded officers at the regimental level who knew nothing about the military. In Kentucky, these same men would have worn stars, or medals. Sherman had plenty of raw manpower at least. Volunteer regiments from Kentucky and other states continued to pour in. For the time being, he used local volunteer groups such as the Kentucky Home Guards, a group that later acquired the nickname "Fireside Rangers." Like the Minutemen of the Revolutionary War, who were ready at a moment's notice, these men came as they were, carrying just their weapons. They were available only for short periods of time, sometimes as little as 10 days. Unfortunately, they also had a tendency to disappear at the slightest hint of danger. In addition, some local squirrel hunters organized themselves into a company of mounted riflemen. One officer commented that the group of so-called soldiers was quite a motley crew.

Sherman was delighted when Secretary of War Simon Cameron and Adjutant General Lorenzo Thomas visited the Department of Cumberland. Thomas and Cameron had been in St. Louis to check out problems in General John C. Frémont's command in Missouri. They stopped briefly in Louisville as they waited for a connecting train back East. With some urging, Sherman convinced Cameron to stay until the next morning so that he could talk to him about the desperate situation in the Army of the Cumberland. Sherman described it as "as bad as bad could be."

At the Galt Hotel, Sherman explained the horrible shape of his army. Desperately needed men and arms had been channeled to other areas of the war, while the Cumberland scarcely got anything. The young men of Kentucky seemed to be flocking to the Confederate camp, leaving only the older men to fight for the Union cause. Sherman believed that in Kentucky the Union was facing a military disaster. He was certain that Confederate general Albert Sidney Johnston could march into Louisville any day and take the city without too much trouble. Cameron was astounded by Sherman's report. The Kentucky delegates in Congress had assured him that the Cumberland had ample manpower and that all it really needed was weaponry and funding.

Sherman figured that he would need an additional 200,000 men to launch an effective offensive. Cameron threw up his hands. "Great God!" he exclaimed. "Where are they to come from?" Sherman suggested that the northwestern states of Iowa, Minnesota, and Wisconsin would be a potential source for troops. At the end of the conversation, Cameron went into action. On the spot, he sent a message by telegraph to army detachments en route to Missouri and had them rerouted to the Army of the Cumberland.

Sherman watched the Confederates at Bowling Green with a sharp eye. He was certain that the Confederates would attack his force at Nolin Creek. The enemy failed to appear, however. Some of Sherman's officers began to wonder whether he was going insane. Worried that the country was headed for ruin, he took little or no sleep and rarely ate. In November, Ellen received an urgent message from Sherman's aide. He wanted her to come to Louisville at once. With General Sherman nearing a breakdown, perhaps she could help ease his stress.

Ellen Sherman left immediately. She knew that insanity ran in Sherman's family, and she was desperately worried about her

General Henry Halleck, known as "Old Brains," was a veteran of the Mexican War and a high-ranking officer in the Union Army during the Civil War. Placed in charge of all Federal troops west of the Appalachian Mountains, Halleck was the one who personally received and welcomed Sherman in St. Louis, Missouri, after the weary soldier was transferred from Kentucky.

husband. Her brother Philemon Ewing and her sons, Willie and Tommy, travelled with her. After a 14-hour train ride, she found her husband in a large, barnlike room blazing with candles. Messengers darted in and out at all hours, bringing details of disaster or threat. There was a couch at one end where Sherman could catch a scrap of sleep from time to time. Ellen was unable to judge the true state of her husband's mind.

Sherman asked to be relieved of his command, and General McClellan agreed to send Don Carlos Buell to take his place. As Sherman waited for Buell to arrive, he received information that led him to believe that the enemy was ready to spring an attack with about 45,000 troops, with their forces growing larger with every passing day. In reality, Sherman was taking snippets of information and piecing them together into the worst possible scenario. When Buell assumed command, he did not see things as being quite so grave. Sherman, of course, thought that Buell was not taking the situation seriously enough.

Sherman was not the only one who saw phantom dangers in Kentucky in the fall of 1861. As Sherman braced for an imaginary attack, Confederate leaders in Columbus did the same. Sherman stayed in Louisville for a week to help Buell settle in. He then reported to Henry Halleck in St. Louis. After a warm welcome, Halleck sent Sherman on an inspection tour of the garrisons west of St. Louis. The general authorized Sherman to assume command if need be. At Seladia, Missouri, Sherman again imagined phantom armies. He took command and issued orders for troops to be sent to Seladia at once. Halleck investigated Sherman's claims and found the orders unnecessary. He called Sherman back to St. Louis and gave him a 20-day leave to get some rest. Halleck reassured Sherman that even a good workhorse needs to be left in the barn from time to time. Ellen hurried to St. Louis and escorted her troubled husband back to Lancaster.

At first, Sherman seemed to improve. Then, the press dealt him a terrible blow. The *Cincinnati Daily Commercial* was the most influential newspaper in the region, boasting nearly 100,000 readers. In December 1861, the *Commercial* printed a story under the headline "General William T. Sherman Insane." The Ewings rallied around Sherman and worked to protect his reputation. Ellen, who was fiercely loyal to her husband, insisted that he had been working heroically in an impossible situation in Kentucky. Overcome with shock and embarrassment, Sherman had to pull himself out from under the black cloud of criticism that shadowed him. He soon faced these shadows with confidence and determination.

Turning Points

In January of 1862, Ellen and her father went to see President Lincoln on behalf of Sherman. With all of the condemning newspaper articles, Sherman was feeling disgraced. But Lincoln had only praise for Sherman, telling Ellen that he had been impressed with Sherman when he was commanding the brigades at Fort Corcoran. In fact, he was sorry he had ever even sent Sherman to Kentucky. At the same time, though, he felt that the state was much safer after Sherman assumed command there. The rough volunteer soldiers had simply made Sherman feel less confident in his army. The only trouble with Sherman, Thomas Ewing pointed out, was that he saw too far and too accurately into the future, and his visions haunted him. In any case, the president had much respect for Sherman.

UNITED STATES VOLUNTEERS ATTACKED BY THE MOB, CORNER OF FIFTH AND WALNUT STREETS, ST. LOUIS, MISSOURI.—[SKETCHED BY M. HASTINGS, ESQ.]

Although stationed in Missouri instead of fighting on the battlefront of the Civil War, Sherman still had to contend with dangerous Confederate sympathizers. Accompanied by his son Willie, Sherman witnessed first-hand the attack on Camp Jackson by a mob of locals supportive of the Southern cause (above). Later in his memoir, Sherman recounted the verbal abuse hurled at the Union Army by the crowd, including cries of "Hurrah for Jeff Davis!"

There was no need to worry. Sherman would have plenty of opportunities to restore his public reputation.

While Ellen was pleading her husband's case in Washington, the Confederate forces in Missouri had fallen back to Springfield and finally scattered. There, General Halleck commanded an army of 80,000 men in a country as hostile as it had been in Mexico. The Confederate force was only about one-fifth of that number, but Missouri had a fair share of Rebel sympathizers who helped the Confederate cause. They destroyed railroads and other lines of communication to cripple the Union Army.

By the end of January 1862, Sherman was back in service. He was stationed at a training camp at the Benton Barracks outside St. Louis, a backwater of the war. Out of the field, Sherman felt almost like an exile. With his still-fragile health, however, he was not yet fit for field command. Halleck explained to Sherman that the position at Benton was not a subordinate rank. Instead, it was the most important post in that department. Halleck reassured Sherman that he soon would take the field again. When that time came, Halleck knew that there was no one he would rather have at his side than Sherman.

Halleck took Sherman into his confidence. He invited him to take part in strategy meetings. One evening, Halleck met with his chief of staff, George W. Cullum, and Sherman. By this time, the Confederates had fortified Columbus, Kentucky, and controlled the Mississippi River southwestward to New Orleans. Westerners were calling for a Union advance down the Mississippi, where Confederate generals Gideon Pillow and Leonidas Polk commanded an army of at least 20,000 men. The Rebel force was heavily armed, with cannon planted securely on the river bluffs.

Halleck pointed to a large map on the table. "Where is the Rebel line?" he asked. Picking up a pencil, Sherman drew a line that ran through Bowling Green, Kentucky; through Fort Henry, on the Tennessee River; and through Fort Donelson, on the Cumberland. "Now," Halleck said, "where is the proper place to break it?" Sherman replied, "Naturally, in the center." Halleck swept a perpendicular line through Sherman's, near the middle. The line followed the course of the Tennessee River. "That's the true line of operations," Halleck said, as quoted in Merrill's *William Tecumseh Sherman*.

Halleck did not favor the idea of sending Union gunboats down the Mississippi River. Instead, he preferred to mount an army-navy operation up the Cumberland and Tennessee rivers, against forts Henry and Donelson—the forts that protected the Union's primary target, Nashville. In early February, Union forces commanded by Ulysses S. Grant boarded transports at Cairo, Illinois, where the Mississippi and Ohio rivers joined. Escorted by Union gunboats, the transports maneuvered into and up the Tennessee River toward Fort Henry.

General Halleck assigned Sherman the command of the District of Cairo—Grant's rear zone—at Paducah, Kentucky. From there, Sherman assembled troops and forwarded them to Grant at the front. He also handled the wounded and guarded Confederate prisoners of war. In Paducah, Sherman put together his own division, a unit that Halleck promised he could take into the field.

Before the Union Army had a chance to attack Fort Henry, heavy firing from the Federals' gunboats pushed the Rebels to surrender. Fort Henry fell to the Union forces on February 6. Ten days later, Grant took Fort Donelson, thereby breaching the Confederate line in Kentucky. With the railroads cut off, the Rebels' supply line was now in jeopardy. Union gunboats continued to push up the Tennessee River as far as Mississippi and Alabama.

On February 16, General Buell took control of Bowling Green, Kentucky. A few days later, Buell's army crossed into Tennessee. Buell took Nashville on February 25. With the Confederate line shattered, Columbus, Kentucky, could no longer be defended. In early March, the Rebel forces pulled out. This retreat tipped the final domino of the tumbling Confederate line in Kentucky.

After months of devastating defeats in the East, news of this victory on the Western Front buoyed Union hopes. Before long, however, the Rebel line reformed further south, in and around Corinth, Mississippi. On Halleck's orders, Grant sent troops to Pittsburgh Landing, Tennessee, on the Tennessee River. Buell and 37,000 soldiers moved to reinforce Grant. Finally, Sherman got a chance to lead an expedition. In mid-March, he led a first wave of troops in a force commanded by Charles F. Smith, a general who had temporarily replaced Grant. Sherman's orders were to lead his division up the Tennessee River to Corinth, where he was to strike the Rebel line and break the Memphis and Charleston Railroad at Burnsville, also in Mississippi. To the east of Burnsville, there stood another important objective—a railroad bridge over Bear Creek.

BECOMING A LEADER

The mission was, literally, a washout. As Union cavalrymen rode through unfamiliar country, the sunlight dimmed. A pelting downpour followed. Soon, streams and gullies swelled with rushing water. The Tennessee River broke its banks, rising an alarming six inches per hour. Several times, men and horses came close to drowning. The cavalry unit had to turn back. Sherman set up base at Pittsburgh Landing, in Tennessee. He then made another attempt to move out, under the cover of night. He moved toward Corinth. He hoped to convert his advance into a railway-and-telegraph-wrecking mission. That did not happen, though. In the middle of the night, Sherman's column ran into a large force of Confederate cavalry. When the alarm sounded in the Rebel camp, Sherman was forced to abort his mission and head back to Pittsburgh Landing.

Undoubtedly, Sherman's men were a bit wary of their commander. The sandy-haired general with the grizzled beard and wild eyes never sat still. His shoulders and hands twitched nervously. At meetings and meals, he always drummed his fingers on the table. His strange idiosyncrasies and erratic behavior were enough to make anyone uneasy in his presence. Most of Sherman's soldiers were fresh out of training. They may have been less than thrilled at the thought of facing combat for the first time under the command of a general who recently had been suspected of insanity.

On March 16, Sherman set out with his division and made camp at Shiloh Church, three miles west of Pittsburgh Landing. The next day, General Grant, who had been reinstated, arrived at Savannah, Tennessee, a short distance downstream from Pittsburgh Landing. Other divisions soon joined the Union forces there. By the beginning of April, about 40,000 more men had arrived. Another 20,000 of Buell's troops soon followed. Meanwhile, a total of 44,000 Confederate troops took up positions in and around Corinth. The stage was set for one of the great battles of the Civil War.

During the first days of April, Sherman's units began to probe the Rebel lines. Then, in the gray light of dawn on Sunday, April 6, the boom of a cannon shook the ground. It heralded a surprise attack by the Confederates. "We were more than surprised," one Illinois officer admitted. "We were astonished!" Grant's forces had established no line or order of battle and had set up no defensive works of any sort. The most exposed position was at Shiloh Church. It was held by the rawest troops, the men under the command of William T. Sherman.

At about 8:00 in the morning, Sherman could see the glistening of bayonets as the enemy infantry attacked the Union's left front. By 10:00, both Sherman's camp and that of General John A. McClernand had been overrun by Confederates. A confusing battle raged all day, in sweltering weather. During the battle, Sherman was wounded twice: He received a buckshot wound in the hand and suffered a bruised shoulder from a musket ball. He also had three horses shot and killed beneath him. All the while, Sherman moved among his troops, trying desperately to keep order.

By nightfall, the Confederates had pushed a mile behind the position that Sherman had held that morning. In the chaotic battle, Yankee soldiers scattered, and men lost touch with their units. Fragments of broken regiments joined whatever command they encountered. Only one of Sherman's brigades remained intact at the end of the day. During the fight, Grant suffered a serious fall from his horse. Because his injury kept him off the field, he was able to offer little help to his floundering soldiers.

Commanding a regiment of the most inexperienced soldiers at the Battle of Shiloh, Sherman and the rest of the Union Army encountered a surprise attack by Confederate forces. The Union fought back the next day, and the Confederacy retreated from Shiloh *(above)*. Past criticisms of Sherman was forgotten as the fearless leader, who was shot twice during the conflict, received praise and a promotion for his performance in battle.

The Confederates finished that first day victorious, but their success came at a high price. Their commanding general, Albert Sidney Johnston, was dead. Bodies of dead Rebels and Yankees littered the battlefield. "The battle . . . was very severe," Sherman wrote to Ellen, as quoted in Brooks and Berlin's *Sherman's Civil War*. "The scenes on this battlefield would have cured anybody of war. Mangled bodies, dead, dying, in every conceivable shape, without heads, legs; and horses!" At the Confederate headquarters near Shiloh Church—a cabin in which Sherman had spent the previous night—General Beauregard assumed command of the Rebel army. Sherman spent most of the night questioning prisoners of war, checking on the wounded, and helping to bury the dead. Meanwhile, General Buell's army arrived at Pittsburgh Landing to strengthen the Union forces.

On the morning of April 7, Grant's reinforced units attacked the Confederates at Shiloh and drove them from the field. Beauregard's men retreated and dug in at Corinth. The Battle of Shiloh ended in a Union victory and redemption for Sherman. General Halleck noted in his report to the War Department, "It is the unanimous opinion here that Brigadier General W.T. Sherman saved the fortune of the day of the 6th and contributed largely to the glorious victory on the 7th. He was in the thickest of the fight on both days." In the same report, Halleck requested that Sherman be promoted to major general. The Union Army—100,000 men strong—moved on to conquer Corinth, which fell at the end of May.

The two days of fighting at Shiloh were a turning point in Sherman's life and military career. His reputation was resurrected, his confidence restored. Years later, he recalled, "That single battle had given me new life." He finally was ready to lead an army.

MEMPHIS UNDER SHERMAN

In July of 1862, Sherman was ordered west to Memphis, Tennessee, which had surrendered to the Union Army at the beginning of June. When Sherman arrived, the people of Memphis were feeling oppressed under the severe Yankee military regime. The city was being run like a prison. To leave town, a civilian needed a pass, which was granted only in a case of urgent necessity. Residents were pressured to take an oath of loyalty to the Union or risk being banished from town. The sale of alcohol was banned, as was the use of Confederate money. This latter rule left the town's economy hard pressed for cash.

On the afternoon of July 20, a group of Memphis citizens stopped Sherman on the street. They wanted to know whether the new commander would put a friendlier kind of military occupation into effect. Sherman replied that Memphis was a conquered city. The people of Memphis were prisoners of war. Maybe they had supported the Union, and maybe they had not. As far as he had heard, however, they had not fought for the Union. Therefore, Memphis, should be treated as a military post.

The people probably felt jarred and nervous after hearing Sherman's stern speech. Sherman did make some changes that eased the lives of residents, however. He reestablished the civil courts and authorities of the city to preserve life, liberty, and property. The military, of course, was superior to civil authority, but at least the local government could go about its regular business and keep the town running. Four days after his arrival, Sherman abolished the system of travel passes. The people of Memphis were free to move in and out of the city with some minor restrictions. All travel had to take place in daylight, and travelers had to use one of five designated roads that passed through military checkpoints. Sherman also lifted the ban on alcohol: He wanted his soldiers to be able to come into town to enjoy some entertainment.

Most of Sherman's time was taken up by an attempt to stop the smuggling of goods out of Memphis and southward to the Confederacy. Although only five designated roads out of town were in use, there were 50 other roads and paths that led into and out of the city. Because it was impossible to keep all of these routes under constant surveillance, smugglers ran rampant. The smugglers were tireless and inventive. They even tried to carry military supplies out of the city in coffins and in the carcasses of hogs. The most critical supply item was salt, which was becoming scarce in many parts of the Confederacy. Salted meat was a staple in the Southern soldier's diet. The merchants of Memphis were ordering so much salt that the Union authorities became suspicious. In August, the U.S. Treasury Department banned any further shipments. To combat the smuggling problem, Sherman stiffened the penalties for people caught smuggling goods. Salt, medicines, and chloroform (used as an anesthetic during surgery) were classified as contraband of war. Anyone convicted of trafficking in these items could be put to death.

AFRICAN-AMERICAN SOLDIERS

Approximately 180,000 African Americans, both free men and runaway slaves, served in the Union Army during the Civil War. Many African Americans also served in the Union Navy. On July 17, 1862, Congress passed two acts that allowed the enlistment of African Americans. Official enroll-ment took place only after September, however, when Lincoln issued the first Emancipation Proclamation.

Most white soldiers and officers believed that black men lacked the courage to fight well. In October 1862, African-American soldiers of the 1st Kansas Colored Volunteers proved them wrong. These soldiers repulsed Confederate attackers at a battle at Island Mound, Missouri. By August 1863, 14 African-American regiments were in the field and ready for service. At the Battle of Port Hudson, Louisiana, on May 27, 1863, African-American soldiers advanced brave-ly over open ground in the face of deadly artillery fire. Although the attack failed, the soldiers proved that they had the courage to withstand the heat of battle.

On July 17, 1863, at Honey Springs, in what is now Oklahoma, the 1st Kansas Colored Volunteers again put up a courageous fight. The Union troops encountered a strong force of Confederates. After a bloody two-hour engage-ment, the Confederates retreated. The 1st Kansas had held the center of the Union line. During the battle, the Kansas regiment advanced to within 50 paces of the Confederate line. The forces exchanged fire for 20 minutes until the

When bands of Rebel guerrilla fighters began to attack Union forces in and around Memphis, Sherman did not hesitate to use harsh measures against them. Civilian resistance and

Confederates broke and ran. After the battle, Union general James G. Blunt wrote, "I never saw such fighting as was done by the [African-American] regiment. . . . The question that [blacks] will fight is settled. Besides, they make better solders in every respect than any troops I have ever had under my command."

Despite the fact that African-American soldiers proved themselves to be brave soldiers, they still faced discrimination. According to the Militia Act of 1862, soldiers of African descent were supposed to receive $10 per month, plus a clothing allowance of $3.50. Many African-American regiments struggled to get the same benefits as white soldiers. Some African-American soldiers were refused any money until June 15, 1864, when Congress granted equal pay for all black soldiers.

African-American soldiers participated in every major campaign of 1864 and 1865 except Sherman's invasion of Georgia. The Battle of New Market Heights, Virginia, was one of the most heroic fights involving African-American soldiers. On September 29, 1864, the African-American division of the 18th Corps charged the Confederate earthworks and rushed up the slopes of the heights. During the hour-long clash, the division suffered tremendous casualties. After the Civil War, 16 African Americans were awarded the Medal of Honor, the nation's highest military honor for individual valor in combat. Fourteen of those men received the honor because of their bravery at New Market Heights.

surprise attacks were frequent and intense. Sherman quickly saw the difficulties faced by a conquering army in a hostile country. Rebel units could maneuver easily in the Memphis area because they did not have to be on guard against the local civilian population. Sherman's force, although much larger than that of the Confederates, was almost ineffective against the flexible, rapid movement of the Rebels.

It became clear to Sherman that every Southern man, woman, and child was set against the Yankee invaders. In a report to General Grant, as recounted in Merrill's *William Tecumseh Sherman*, Sherman wrote, "We cannot change the hearts of the people of the South, but we can make war so terrible that they will realize the fact that, however brave and gallant and devoted to their country, still they are mortal and should exhaust all peaceful remedies before they fly to war." Sherman believed that although Southerners "cannot be made to love us, they can be made to fear us." In a letter to his daughter Minnie, quoted in *Sherman's Civil War*, he wrote, "I have been forced to turn families out of their houses and homes and force them to go to a strange land, because of their hostility. . . . Pray every night that this war may end." He added, "Every day I meet old friends who would now shoot me dead if I were to go outside Camp and who look at me as a brutal wretch."

In the late summer of 1862, the question of slavery became an important factor in the war. Should slaves in the Rebel states be freed? Northern abolitionists wanted the slaves to be freed for moral reasons. There also was an important military argument to be made for emancipation, however. The Southern economy was built on slavery. If the slaves were to be freed, the Southern economy would take a fatal blow. In addition, fleeing slaves would cause mass confusion in the Confederate states. From the beginning of the war, slaves were considered contraband. As valuable commodities, they were critical to the Confederate war effort and could flee to Union states or be taken from Confederates.

For the most part, Sherman stayed neutral in the slavery debate. He did not disturb the relationship between slave and slaveholder, but he did nothing to return runaways. On September 22, 1862, President Lincoln issued a preliminary Emancipation Proclamation. It notified the Confederate states that their slaves would be considered free as of January 1, 1863. Sherman looked ahead to the turmoil that would follow. "Are we to feed all the [African-American] men, women, and children?" he said. Freedom might be a grand idea, Sherman reflected, "but freedom don't clothe them, feed them, and shelter them."

In late autumn, when most of the Sherman children were in school at Notre Dame, Indiana, Ellen and Tommy visited Memphis. During the past several months, Sherman had thought often about his family, and it pained him to be so far away from them for so long. Ellen was pleased to find her husband healthy and cheerful, even if he was a bit too thin and wore a few more wrinkles. During the visit, the soldiers grew quite fond of Tommy. The tailor for one of the companies made him a uniform, complete with a corporal's stripes.

At about this time, General McClernand contacted President Lincoln. A former Democratic congressman from Illinois, McClernand commanded a volunteer unit with a good combat record. He was an ambitious general and had a firm grasp of Midwestern politics. He realized that a political crisis had been mounting in the prairie states. After a year and a half of fighting, the professional Union soldiers had been unable to break the Rebel barriers on the Mississippi River. Because the states of the Midwest depended on river trade, the failure to open up the Mississippi could destroy the region's desire to support the Union war effort. The general had a plan in mind to deal with this situation, but he needed the president's approval.

The Fight for Mississippi

The Mississippi River was the key to the war, and Vicksburg, Mississippi, was the key to the Mississippi River. The city stood on a hairpin curve below fortified bluffs, and it was nearly impossible to send transports past the Confederate guns that were located there. In the fall of 1862, the Rebels still held firm control of the river from Vicksburg to Baton Rouge, Louisiana. Communication lines and supply routes running east and west ran through this sector. If the Union could take control of Vicksburg, it could deal a crippling blow to the Confederacy.

McClernand wanted Lincoln's permission to build an army in Illinois. With this force, he planned to go down the Mississippi River, capture Vicksburg, and then head eastward toward Atlanta or westward into Texas. The idea seemed like a good one, especially because Union forces at New Orleans that would be moving up the river at the same time could serve as reinforcements in Vicksburg. Secretary of War Edwin M. Stanton drew up the orders. General McClernand was to take command of the men who remained in Indiana, Illinois, and Iowa, and was to recruit reinforcements. These forces were to report to Sherman in Memphis before moving against Vicksburg.

In early December 1862, Sherman met with Grant at Oxford, Mississippi, where the two generals talked about the Mississippi River campaign. Because Grant had little patience for politicians turned soldiers like McClernand, he assigned Sherman to take command of the Vicksburg expedition. Sherman was to lead a force of 40,000 troops on transports and Union gunboats. The men were to land on the banks of the Yazoo River, which empties into the Mississippi north of Vicksburg. From there, they would swing inland and strike Vicksburg from the rear, on the city's land side. At the same time, Grant and his troops were to move on Vicksburg by way of Grenada, Mississippi, keeping Confederate general John C. Pemberton's army away from the city and its defenses. General Nathaniel P. Banks and his army, aided by Union gunboats, were to steam up the Mississippi toward Vicksburg.

The campaign was extremely hazardous. The Confederate line of defense, of which Vicksburg was the center, faced the river. On the right side of the line, the Confederates held a strongly fortified position on the Yazoo River at Haynes Bluff, 12 miles from Vicksburg. The left side of the Rebel line was on the Mississippi, at Grand Gulf, 60 miles below Vicksburg by river, but just 30 miles by land. Vicksburg was fortified by land and water and was within telegraphic and railroad reach of Meridian, Mississippi; Mobile, Alabama; and Grenada, where Pemberton commanded his large Confederate force.

By the time Sherman got back to Memphis from Oxford, McClernand had already sent down 49 regiments of infantry from Indiana and Illinois. At Memphis, Sherman met with Admiral David Dixon Porter for the first time. Sherman explained the plans for the entire mission. Porter, who thought Sherman was a nervous, restless man, immediately noticed a major difference between Sherman and Grant. Grant usually left the details to others, whereas Sherman personally attended to all of the details of the mission.

On December 20, troops, horses, mules, wagons, and artillery set off for Vicksburg on the transport *Forest Queen* and 70 other steamers. Four days later, the flotilla arrived at Helena, Arkansas, where General Frederick Steele's division joined the expedition. Seven thousand Union soldiers landed at Milliken's Bend, Louisiana, stormed to Monroe, Louisiana, and tore up 30 miles of railroad track. The mission temporarily halted communications between Vicksburg and the wealthy areas of Texas that supplied the city.

Meanwhile, although Sherman did not know it at the time, Confederate forces were cutting Grant and his army off from all communications and forcing Grant to return to his initial point of departure. After Grant's retreat, General Pemberton fell back to Vicksburg. There, he concentrated an additional 12,000 men to wage battle against Sherman's now unsupported army. Sherman was unaware that General Banks was confined to a hospital bed in New Orleans and could not move up the Mississippi as planned.

On December 26, Sherman's expedition steamed up the Yazoo River and went ashore on a flat strip of land beneath the steep cliffs of Walnut Hills, on the river side of which Vicksburg stood. For the next two days, the Union troops inched forward, skirmishing with Pemberton's units, until they reached a broad bayou at the foot of Chickasaw Bluffs. Beyond this point, the Union troops faced a section of land lined with rifle pits (or trenches) and cannon, and Confederate batteries crowned the bluffs behind them. There, on the riverbank, Sherman waited impatiently for news about Grant. The only sound for miles

Hoping to capture Vicksburg, Mississippi, a major Confederate stronghold along the Mississippi River, Union leader Ulysses S. Grant devised an offensive campaign with the help of Sherman. While the siege did not go exactly as planned, Union forces eventually were able to seize the city, guaranteeing them the use of a major supply route that ran through the heart of the South. *Above*, the Battle of Vicksburg.

around was the chug of enemy trains, loaded with Confederate reinforcements enroute to Vicksburg.

To delay the attack any longer would destroy any chance the Union still had of victory. So, on December 29, Sherman launched the first assault. The Confederates lashed back with rigorous firepower. One Union brigade moved across the bayou below Chickasaw Bluffs and found shelter under the bank. Another unit crossed the bayou farther down. The men held these posts until darkness fell, after which they withdrew. The day had been a disaster. By the end of the battle, 175 Union soldiers were dead, another 930 were wounded, and more than 700 were missing. Dejected and exhausted, Sherman boarded Porter's flagship *Blackhawk*, still wondering what had happened to Grant and Banks.

On the following day, Sherman assembled a fresh detachment to try one more landing effort, this time farther down from Vicksburg. The attack never took place, though. On New Year's morning 1863, a dense fog prevented any movement up or down the river. The next day, more Confederate troops dotted the bluffs. Through sheets of pouring rain, Sherman scanned the hills in disgust. Any chance of surprise had long since passed, and he knew that his army could not take Vicksburg unassisted. Sherman and his troops made a swift retreat to Milliken's Bend.

By January 1863, the faces of Northerners held expressions of doom and gloom. Twenty months had passed since Fort Sumter, and there had been more Union defeats than victories. In Tennessee, General Rosecrans's Army of the Cumberland had fought a savage battle with Braxton Bragg's Confederate forces. It was a drawn fight, with no winner or loser. In the East, the Army of the Potomac, under General Ambrose E. Burnside, had repeatedly been whipped by the Confederates under Robert E. Lee.

As the days slipped by, General McClernand still was unable to come up with a definite plan to open up the Mississippi and cut through to the Gulf of Mexico. For now, he decided that there was nothing Union forces could do at Vicksburg. Sherman suggested that the army turn around, move 50 miles up the Arkansas River, and attack Arkansas Post, also known as Fort Hindman. McClernand like the idea. Soon, Porter's gunboats and army transports were maneuvering up the Mississippi toward the mouth of the Arkansas River.

In the early morning of January 8, Union forces reached the mouth of the White River. The next day, they turned from the Mississippi into the broad Arkansas River. After a two-day assault, the Union Army captured Arkansas Post. There,

Sherman and McClernand received new orders. The Western armies under Grant were being regrouped into five corps. The 13th was to be commanded by McClernand. In Middle Tennessee, the 14th was under George H. Thomas. Near Memphis, Stephen A. Hurlburt commanded the 16th. In western Tennessee, the 17th was under James McPherson. Sherman was to assume command of the 15th. Together, these corps would launch new operations against Vicksburg.

VICTORY AT LAST

In April 1863, Union forces were still before Vicksburg, but with a new plan. Admiral Porter's ironclads and a half-dozen transports were to run past the enemy batteries at Vicksburg while Grant's army marched down the Louisiana side of the Mississippi to a point opposite Grand Gulf. There, Grant's men were to cross the river on transports, storm the Grand Gulf area, and then threaten the cities of Jackson and Vicksburg, Mississippi, from the south. Sherman was against this plan because he foresaw that the Union's supply line would be precarious once the army crossed the Mississippi. Sherman believed that the unsuccessful December 1862 plan, if correctly executed, stood a better chance of breeching the Confederate defenses. Grant disagreed.

In mid-April, Porter's fleet of ironclads and transports successfully passed the guns of Vicksburg. The Union's land forces then began their march across the Louisiana countryside. On April 29, however, Porter's gunboats failed to destroy the defensive works on the bluff at Grand Gulf. Meanwhile, the army continued to push southward to Bruinsburg, Mississippi.

At dawn on April 30, General McClernand's forces started to move across the Mississippi on transports. Sherman and his men were ready to follow Grant and the rest of the army downriver. Suddenly, the orders were altered. Some of Sherman's units were to attack Haynes Bluff, on the Yazoo, to divert the enemy's attention from Grant's forces.

A week later, after leading the assault on Haynes Bluff, Sherman and his divisions rejoined Grant and the rest of the force downriver. Grant's strategy was to head for Vicksburg with his army of 41,000 troops through Jackson, the capital of Mississippi, which was located to the east. At Jackson, Grant would face General Joseph Johnston's force of 15,000 men. At Vicksburg, he would face General Pemberton's army of 40,000.

When Grant reached Jackson, the Confederates made a hasty retreat. Sherman's men stayed in Jackson just long enough to tear up the railroads, arsenals, a government foundry, the penitentiary, and a cotton factory. Union soldiers also set fire to other buildings, including a Catholic church and the Confederate Hotel. At this point, Sherman began to gain the reputation of a modern Attila—a general both ruthless and destructive.

From Jackson, Grant turned west. He marched back toward the Mississippi and placed his troops between those of Pemberton and Johnston. On May 16 and 17, Union troops clashed with Pemberton's army at Champion's Hill and Big Black River Bridge. Defeated, the Confederate force fell back to Vicksburg.

On May 19 and 22, Grant's army failed to penetrate the Confederate defenses at Vicksburg. Grant settled in for a long siege. For more than six weeks, the Yankees and the Rebels battled each other from a distance of 600 yards or less. Less than a month earlier, Sherman had been skeptical of Grant's plan. Grant had managed to pull it off, though. By doing so won Sherman's ultimate respect and admiration.

For weeks, Union guns pounded Vicksburg. Early each morning, Sherman supervised the firing of his artillery, which tore the city to shreds.

On July 3, 1863, General Pemberton began negotiations for the surrender of Vicksburg. Fittingly, the Union Army made its triumphant march down the road toward the fallen city on the Fourth of July, as the army bands played "Yankee Doodle."

Soon afterward, the Union forces at Vicksburg received news from the East: General George Meade and the Army of the Potomac had won a glorious victory at Gettysburg and chased Lee's Confederate army into a full retreat. To the south, along the Mississippi, Confederate-held Port Hudson, Louisiana, had surrendered to General Bank's force. The Mississippi River was open to Union commerce all the way to the Gulf of Mexico.

DOORWAY TO GEORGIA

In sweltering afternoon heat and thick dust, Sherman's men crossed the Big Black River and forced General Johnston's retreating army to take refuge behind their earthworks at Jackson. On July 9, Sherman announced that the state capital was besieged. The Union artillery opened fire. Other Yankee detachments began to destroy railroads and strip the country-side of corn, cattle, hogs, sheep, and poultry. Johnston's Rebel army made a full retreat. As Union soldiers moved into Jackson, the troops set businesses ablaze, burned down some of the finest houses, and looted homes. Throughout his life, Sherman had a high sense of justice, and he found anarchy in any form appalling. Despite his beliefs, he was entirely committed to the practice of destroying enemy resources. In his mind, to lay waste to enemy countryside was to bring a swift end to a war.

On July 22, Sherman issued orders for his division to return to their camps on the Big Black River for a much-needed rest. He urged Ellen to bring the children to the camp, and in mid-August she arrived with the four oldest children. During their visit, little Willie became ill with typhoid. On October 3, on the way back to Lancaster, he took his final breath. William Ewing Sherman received a full military funeral in Memphis. The battalion of the 13th United States Regulars escorted the casket from the Gayoso House to the steamboat *Grey Eagle*, which carried the family upriver. For weeks, Sherman was grief–stricken. He was haunted by Willie's death. Undoubtedly, he partially blamed himself for begging the family to come to visit.

While Sherman's army sat idle in camp, on other fronts the war was entering a new phase. The Union's Army of the Cumberland had moved against the Confederate forces of General Bragg in Tennessee, but the Yankees were repelled at Chickamauga Creek. The remnants of the Union Army dug in at Chattanooga to endure Bragg's siege. Meanwhile, the Confederates took control of Missionary Ridge, which overlooked Chattanooga, and occupied Lookout Mountain, west of the city. Union reinforcements were rushed in from the East, and Halleck sent word to Grant to dispatch a unit at once to Chattanooga. Grant ordered Sherman to lead the bulk of his corps from the Big Black River into eastern Tennessee, through Memphis. On Sunday, October 11, Sherman set off for Chattanooga.

On November 15, Sherman arrived in Chattanooga. There, with Grant and generals George H. Thomas and William F. Smith, he inspected the city's defenses. To the east, enemy tents perched all along the slope of Missionary Ridge, with lines of trenches clearly visible. General Bragg's Confederate army faced Chattanooga in a crescent-shaped position, with one point touching the Tennessee River and the southern side of the city. Upstream, the Rebels controlled Tunnel Hill; downstream, they commanded Lookout Mountain. In the center of the crescent was Missionary Ridge, which rose 500 feet above the plain.

Bragg's defenses seemed nearly impenetrable. To break the Confederate stranglehold on Chattanooga, Grant developed a three-pronged plan of attack. General Joseph Hooker was to attack Lookout Mountain. Sherman was to move up the Tennessee River, cross over, and strike the upper end of Missionary Ridge. Meanwhile, Thomas's army was to launch an assault on the center.

On November 23, Sherman got his divisions over to the hills. The next day, he drove the enemy off the northern end of Missionary Ridge. Meanwhile, General Hooker, outnumbering his opponent almost six to one, easily captured Lookout

The Army of the Cumberland *(above)* fought successfully at the Battle of Chattanooga in Tennessee, only to be repelled when trying to overtake nearby Chickamauga. Forced to retreat, the Union soldiers allowed Confederate troops to seize important battle positions, like Lookout Mountain. General Ulysses S. Grant ordered additional men to assist the Army of the Cumberland, including a regiment led by Sherman.

Mountain. At dawn on November 25, Sherman led another attack. From the outer fringes of the Tunnel Hill fortification, the Confederates suddenly pounced on the right rear of the Union flank. The Yankees fell back in disorder but quickly regrouped. Believing that the Confederate force in front of him was being reinforced, Sherman called for more troops. Some of Thomas's regiments rushed to Sherman's aid, but Sherman still could not break the Rebel line. At about three that afternoon, Sherman noticed the white smoke that indicated a line of musket fire in the distance. At last, Thomas was moving against the center of the Confederate line. His 18,000 Union soldiers were advancing toward towering Missionary Ridge in one of the most dramatic charges of the entire war. Suddenly, Rebel guns that had been trained on Sherman's forces all day swung in a different direction. Thomas's army swept up Missionary Ridge and broke the center of the Confederate line. Bragg's men turned in full retreat, and Chattanooga was safe from siege.

The victory at Chattanooga was of vital importance. Now, the Union had cut off the routes that allowed the Confederacy's critical supplies of iron ore and coal to reach the Georgia iron mills. Also, Chattanooga gave the Union a doorway into Georgia.

March to the Sea

In the spring of 1864, President Lincoln called Grant back East to take command of all the Union armies. Sherman was appointed head of the Military Division of the Mississippi. As April gave way to May, Sherman invaded the state of Georgia with three armies. At the start of September, when he arrived in Atlanta, Sherman had accomplished all of his assigned duties except that of destroying the Confederate Army.

Confederate general John Hood had fled Atlanta and marched his army southward. Sherman's men pursued Hood for 30 miles and then returned to the city. Hood proceeded to attack the Union's line of railroad communications that ran to Chattanooga. Although Sherman worked to protect these lines, he made no real attempt to battle Hood. He argued that he could never run down the Confederates, and he refused to scramble all over the state on a wild-goose chase. In truth, he was not interested in John Hood. Sherman was setting into motion his own brilliant plan of attack. He knew that, in war, the advantage always turns to whoever acts with speed, surprise, and resolution.

In the original plan, Sherman was to hold Atlanta with a detachment and strike off for the Atlantic Coast with the rest of his force. On the way, his army was to occupy key positions on the two railroads that ran east to west across the state of Georgia. The object of this move was to split the Confederacy. Sherman realized, however, that his command would not be able to keep the supply line—a railroad that ran from Nashville to Atlanta through Chattanooga—open for long against the superior Confederate cavalry. He altered his plans. His new strategy was one of destruction, beginning in Atlanta and ending at the state capital of Milledgeville. Sherman's march would force Hood to move to protect either Augusta, to the north, or Macon, to the south; both were key industrial cities. Sherman planned to capture whichever city was left undefended and, after its destruction, advance on the other.

Such a march would require Sherman's army to move rapidly through Georgia and live off the land. The impact on the South would be great. "Instead of being on the defensive, I would be on the offensive," Sherman reasoned with Grant. "Instead of guessing at what [Hood] means to do, he would have to guess at my plans."

On October 1, 1864, Sherman telegraphed Grant to suggest that General Thomas and his force be sent to deal with Hood. Meanwhile, Sherman planned to march the rest of his army to the coastal city of Savannah, destroying railroads and inflicting irreparable damage along the way. Grant wired his approval of this March to the Sea. At once, Sherman went to work to prepare for the 300-mile march. He divided his thoroughly equipped army, which now numbered 60,000 men, into four corps that made up a right wing and a left wing. The left

Sherman and Ulysses S. Grant believed that the devastating war would end only if the Confederate Army's capacity for warfare was decisively broken. Sherman ordered his troops to destroy much of the city on their way into and out of Atlanta. Yet, this paled in comparison to the damage done by Union forces in Sherman's next campaign, the March to the Sea. Here, Sherman *(center, leaning on gun in black hat)* is with his staff at Federal Fort No. 7 in Atlanta.

wing, consisting of the 14th and 20th Corps, was commanded by West Point graduate Major General Henry W. Slocum. This force later was renamed the Army of Georgia. The right wing, made up of the 15th and 17th Corps, was under the command of Major General O.O. Howard, another West Point graduate. It later became known as the Army of the Tennessee. The cavalry, under Brigadier General Judson Kilpatrick, reported directly to Sherman.

Without divulging their ultimate destination, Sherman issued a special field order for the troops. The army was to forage the countryside but not to enter homes. During halts, the troops could gather potatoes and other vegetables and drive in livestock. Horses, mules, and wagons could be freely seized. All along the way, the army was to destroy railroad tracks, mills, and factories, thereby enforcing a relentless devastation.

On November 14, Sherman's Engineer Corps began the task of destruction in Atlanta. They demolished the railroad depot, machine shops, and any facility that might aid the Confederates. That night, the heart of Atlanta became a raging inferno as one explosion after another detonated. Blasts of sparks and fire spit upward against a black sky. On November 16, Sherman and his 60,000 men moved out of Atlanta. The fateful march had begun.

Following a line of march that ran southeastward between Macon and Augusta, Sherman's army carved a 60-mile-wide swath of devastation through the heartland of the Confederacy. As the Union divisions advanced through the Georgia countryside, bridges were demolished and railroad cars dismantled. Plumes of smoke billowed by day, and pillars of fire blazed by night. Whatever the soldiers could not bring with them, they burned. Foraging was carried out with military precision. Each brigade dispatched a party of 50 men on foot. The men returned later, on horseback, driving cattle, mules, and horses and hauling wagons loaded with smoked bacon, turkeys, chickens, ducks, sacks of cornmeal, jugs of molasses, and piles of sweet potatoes.

On November 16, Sherman stood on a hill just east of Atlanta to gaze across the Georgia countryside. To the southeast, he could see the glint of the rifle barrels from the men of the Army of the Tennessee. Directly in front of him, he watched the men of the 14th Corps as they marched along the road to the east. To the rear, the city of Atlanta lay in smoldering ruins, coughing up clouds of smoke. For the first time since the war began, three and a half years earlier, Sherman sensed that victory was within the Union's grasp.

At Decatur, just outside Atlanta, the 14th and 20th Corps took separate roads. The 20th pushed southeastward to Madison and swung through Eatonton into the capital, Milledgeville. Meanwhile, the 14th took a much more direct route to the capital. After battering Milledgeville, the two corps continued down separate roads. Both columns devastated towns along the way, including Sandersville, Louisville, and Millen. The men continued to destroy or confiscate anything of military value: railroad tracks, cotton mills, machinery, food supplies, horses, mules, and much more. Confederate resistance was almost nonexistent on the army's left wing until it approached Savannah, where it encountered Rebel troops under the command of Lieutenant General William Hardee.

The army's right wing also marched along separate roads to the south, toward Macon. The troops swept through the towns of McDonough, Jackson, and Clinton. North of Macon, at Griswoldville, a reinforced brigade from the 15th Corps pushed back an assault by Georgia militiamen, inflicting heavy losses on the Confederates. Other than this assault, the right wing, like the left, met little opposition along the way. North of Macon, the right wing continued along various roads, pummeling the towns of Irwinton, Millen, and Statesborough and tearing up the Georgia Central Railroad all the way from Macon to Savannah. Early in the campaign, the Union cavalry covered the flanks of the right wing. Later, near Milledgeville, it shifted over to the left wing.

About 13,000 Confederate troops under William Hardee were entrenched around Savannah. The Rebel force prepared to stop Sherman's approaching army. Despite Sherman's threats to the safety of the people in the city, Hardee refused to surrender. He still had one road—the Union Causeway—open across a bridge that spanned the Savannah River and gave access to neighboring South Carolina.

The Union's Henry Slocum suggested to Sherman that he send the 20th Corps across the Savannah River to close the road and cut off Hardee's one chance to retreat. Sherman refused to approve the plan. For one thing, he was unable to ensure the safety of his troops once they were across the river. More importantly, he needed them if the Union Army launched an attack. A better plan, Sherman believed, was to bring in part of Major General John Foster's command from

"FORTY ACRES AND A MULE"

As Union soldiers pushed deeper into Georgia, tens of thousands of freed slaves left their plantations to follow General William Tecumseh Sherman's army. From all directions, they flocked to his columns. Their bony horses pulled wagons piled with chests, quilts, and iron kettles. Some of them pushed wheelbarrows or pulled handcarts. Although their desperate condition concerned Sherman, he could not afford to devote time and energy to caring for refugees.

On January 16, 1865, Sherman issued Special Field Orders, No. 15. This temporary plan granted each freed family 40 acres of tillable land on coastal islands and along the coast of Georgia. In addition, the army granted its unneeded mules to these African-American settlers. News of these grants of "40 acres and a mule" spread like wildfire. Freed slaves saw the grants as proof that emancipation finally would give them a piece of the land on which they had worked for so long. The orders were in effect for only one year.

the coastal islands of South Carolina to block the Savannah River causeway. Sherman traveled by sea to Hilton Head, South Carolina, to discuss the plan with Foster. While Sherman was on the island, Hardee abandoned Savannah and escaped with his forces.

Sherman captured Savannah on December 21, 1864. He wrote to President Lincoln to tell him the good news. "I beg to present you as a Christmas gift the city of Savannah," he wrote, "with 150 heavy guns and plenty of ammunition and also about 25,000 bales of cotton." Three weeks after the fall of Savannah, Sherman prepared to embark on a second campaign of destruction. This time he planned to head northward, through the Carolinas.

REVENGE: THE CAROLINAS CAMPAIGN

"With Savannah in our possession," Sherman told Grant, as recounted in Merrill's *William Tecumseh Sherman*, "we can punish South Carolina as she deserves." From Fort Sumter onward, many Northerners blamed South Carolina—the first state to secede—for starting the war and were eager to inflict some revenge. "I almost tremble for [South Carolina]," Sherman wrote, "but feel she deserves all that seems in store for her."

On January 21, 1865, Sherman sent the 17th Corps and three divisions of the 15th Corps by sea to Beaufort, South Carolina, to open the Carolinas campaign. In his plan, the right wing was to advance inland and outflank the Confederate forces, which had flooded fields and prepared fortifications to stop the Union advance. Once again, Sherman split his four corps and had them travel by separate roads. The Union forces met with little resistance. As they had done in Georgia, Sherman's army lived off the land. They also carried out a policy of devastation that exceeded that of the Savannah campaign. The Army of Georgia headed across the South Carolina border into Fayetteville, North Carolina, demolishing the South Carolina towns of Blackville and Lexington along the way.

With Georgia fully conquered, Sherman led his men northward toward the Carolinas. Determined to punish South Carolina for being the first state to secede, Sherman's men burned and pillaged everything in sight. Unable to muster up any type of defense, Southern General Johnston remarked, "I made up my mind that there had been no such army in existence since the days of Julius Caesar." *Above*, a view of Charleston, South Carolina, and the aftermath of Sherman's forces.

On the other flank, the Army of the Tennessee, led by O.O. Howard, drove through the towns of Pocotaligo and Orangeburg and advanced to the South Carolina state capital, Columbia. On February 17, Union forces occupied Columbia, and the Yankee soldiers pillaged and plundered throughout the night. Sherman moved out of Columbia on February 21. The next towns along his route—Winnsboro, Camden, and Cheraw—suffered similar fates at the hands of the Union Army. When the army entered North Carolina, the fire of revenge was extinguished. The troops seemed to understand that they were marching into a state where the citizens had been more reluctant to leave the Union than the residents of South Carolina had been. On March 11, Fayetteville surrendered.

Sherman's army moved on toward Goldsboro, North Carolina. Along the way, Confederate general Joseph Johnston came close to overwhelming Sherman's forces at Bentonville. Although victorious, the Yankee army did not pursue the enemy. Instead, Sherman advanced to Goldsboro.

Meanwhile, the Confederates were working desperately to amass all available troops to stop the Union advance. To command this army, Confederate president Jefferson Davis appointed Sherman's rival Joseph Johnston. With about 16,000 infantrymen and artillerymen and a cavalry force of 7,000, Johnston hoped to crush one of Sherman's wings. Marching toward Goldsboro, Sherman planned to join another 40,000 Union troops under Major General John M. Schofield. The two Union wings took different roads; at one stage of the advance, they were separated by a full day's march. It was at this vulnerable point that Johnston made his move on Sherman's left wing.

On March 16, a corps of Confederate troops under Hardee launched a battle near Averasborough, North Carolina, that was intended to delay the Union Army. This fight gave Johnston enough time to concentrate his forces at the precise location where Sherman's columns were a day's march apart. Early on the afternoon of March 19, Confederate infantrymen blasted through parts of the 14th and 20th Corps at Bentonville. Another division of Union troops held firm, even though the Rebels struck them from both the front and the rear. Reinforcements from the 20th Corps rushed to the scene and secured the center and left flanks of the Union line.

Despite repeated assaults, the Confederates could not break the Union line. In the late afternoon, Johnston broke off the attack. The following morning, the Army of Tennessee reached the battle site. Facing overwhelming odds, Johnston managed to retain his position. On March 21, however, a Union attack nearly cut off his line of retreat. That night, the Confederates fell back. Three days later, Sherman's army reached Goldsboro.

After a 17-day rest, Sherman's army—which now consisted of the Army of Georgia, the Army of the Tennessee, and Schofield's two corps in the center—set out in search of Johnston's army. Originally, Grant had wanted Sherman to push on into Virginia. Several days before, Grant wired Sherman to tell him that Richmond, Virginia, the Confederate capital, had fallen, and that Lee's army was on the run. Sherman's new target was to be Johnston's army. On April 10, Sherman broke camp. Two days later, Raleigh, the capital of North Carolina, fell to Judson Kilpatrick's Union cavalry. Sherman's drive through the Carolinas was bold, imaginative, and masterfully executed. On that same day—April 12, 1865—Sherman received the glorious news from Grant at Appomattox Court House, Virginia, that Lee had surrendered. The Union had won the war.

A PUSH FOR PEACE

Tensions continued even after Lee's surrender. Just two days later, on April 14, 1865, as he attended a play at Ford's Theatre in Washington, President Abraham Lincoln was assassinated by actor and Confederate sympathizer John Wilkes Booth. On April 18, generals Sherman and Johnston met to discuss peace. Sherman offered terms that restored the South to a status close to that of its prewar days. His mild negotiations proved that his practice of "hard war" was strategic, not vindictive. Sherman tried to arrange a plan that would allow North and South to live side by side in peace. Recognizing that Southerners had suffered terribly during the war, he wanted to make the transition back into the Union a smooth one.

Sherman's actions, however noble, enraged Andrew Johnson, who had ascended to the presidency after Lincoln's assassination. Not only had Sherman promoted a policy that all

Despite his brutal March to the Sea Campaign, Sherman was hesitant to impose punishing terms for Confederate general Joseph E. Johnston and the two negotiated a surrender agreement favorable to the South *(above)*. Sherman created a peace treaty based on what he believed were fair terms, but his kindness towards the Confederacy was not well received in the wake of Lincoln's assassination.

but acknowledged the Confederacy, he also had left the South armed. Moreover, Sherman had snatched the task of Southern Reconstruction from the hands of Congress and the president and taken on the bold and crucial business himself. In the North, people were demanding that the South be punished for the war. Sherman's terms for peace would never be acceptable.

President Johnson immediately rejected Sherman's peace proposal. He told Secretary of War Edwin M. Stanton to tell Sherman to resume hostilities against General Johnston. As the president saw it, they were still at war. As soon as news of Sherman's agreements with Johnston leaked to the public, Stanton issued a statement to the newspapers in which he referred to Sherman as corrupt and a traitor.

Sherman calmly accepted his orders from Stanton. He dutifully obeyed but staunchly insisted that his own plan was right, honest, and fair. On April 26, he met again with Johnston to present new terms—terms that were brief and simple, like those that Grant had presented to Lee at Appomattox. At this point, Sherman had been completely relieved from the task of reconstructing the South.

When Sherman picked up a five-day-old newspaper and read Stanton's merciless attack on his character and loyalty, he flew into a rage. He wrote to Grant, saying,

> I have never in my life questioned or disobeyed an order though many and many a time I have risked my life, my health and reputation in obeying orders or even hints to execute plans and purposes not to my liking. . . . It is true that non-combatants, men who sleep in comfort & security whilst we watch on the distant Lines are better able to judge than we poor soldiers, who rarely see a newspaper, hardly can hear from our families, or stop long enough to draw our pay. I envy not the task of reconstruction, and am delighted that the Secretary of War has relieved me of it.

On May 30, Sherman wrote a farewell to his men. In his statement, he recounted their many triumphs and acknowledged their hard work and discipline. "Our work is done," he said, "the War is over, and our Government stands vindicated before the world by the joint action of the Volunteer Armies of the United States." The next day, with Ellen, Tommy, and Ellen's father, Thomas Ewing, he boarded a train for New York. At the age of 45, he had reached the height of military fame and glory. He had been released from the rigors of war, and he desperately wanted to build a close relationship with his family after four long, hard years of separation. In 1864, Ellen had given birth to another baby boy, named Charles. Sherman believed that he now had the chance to get to know his new son. From New York, the family traveled home to Lancaster, Ohio.

Sherman's time in Lancaster was short lived. He was called to Chicago to meet with General Grant and learn his new assignment. The postwar nation had been divided into military divisions, departments, and districts, which were to be commanded by lieutenant, major, and brigadier generals. Sherman's command was to be the Division of the Missouri. It covered the entire Great Plains region and had its headquarters in St. Louis. As in the past, Sherman went ahead to his new post without Ellen and the children. Once there, he bought a grand, red-brick house on Garrison Avenue known as the Nicholson House. Ellen and the children soon arrived, and the Shermans settled in with bright hopes for future happiness.

Years of Peace

The immediate postwar period left the South stunned and shattered, and Southerners reacted with shock and bewilderment. The men who had engineered the war—and lost it—saw great empires of cotton, rice, tobacco, and sugar collapse. An entire class of people suddenly found itself stripped of property and wealth. Millions of former slaves were free. Once-great plantations stood empty and abandoned. Those that had stood in Sherman's path lay in ruins. The jagged remains of walls and the charred skeletons of buildings rose out of the ashes.

Meanwhile, in St. Louis, Sherman's primary problem was the protection of frontier settlers from hostile American Indians. The Division of the Missouri posed challenges that Sherman was not particularly well equipped to meet. The

Indians turned out to be one of Sherman's toughest opponents yet. They were lean, hardened, and determined to hold on to their lands. The American Indians needed few supplies and rode fine horses. They possessed an outstanding ability to camouflage their presence and ride extraordinary distances to fight at places of their own choosing. Their hit-and-run attacks were unpredictable and incredibly effective.

In the 1860s, the Western frontier was a vast, unsettled country. The region was 2,000 miles long and 600 miles wide. The American Indian groups were so scattered that no single army could defeat them. The U.S. Army seemed to get swallowed up in a sea of prairie. In a letter to Thomas Ewing, Sherman wrote, "No amount of men [can] guard the long lines of the frontier." Sherman believed that the only way to deal with the American Indian problem was to settle the land in the usual way and eventually defeat each group of American Indians as the opportunity arose. Sherman was well aware that the American Indians' way of life suffered at the hands of settlers and under the broken treaties drawn up by American politicians. Sadly, however, like many other Americans at the time, Sherman saw the American Indians as an inferior race that was destined to be controlled by white people.

War with the American Indians was almost constant. Between 1865 and 1890, the U.S. Army engaged in 948 battles with various groups. Most of these battles involved small numbers of combatants. In the encounter at Little Big Horn in 1876—the battle in which General George A. Custer made his famous last stand—only part of a single regiment of U.S. Cavalry fought against the Lakota Sioux.

Sherman's work in the Division of the Missouri was interrupted frequently by other assignments. In the late 1860s, he was drawn into political conflicts in Washington, D.C. President Johnson and Congress were at odds over Reconstruction in the South. Johnson—a Southerner—had come to favor a mild

Sherman was relocated to St. Louis when he was assigned to establish law and order in the Division of Missouri after the Civil War. Set on the frontier, Sherman was tasked with protecting U.S. settlers from threats of American Indian attacks. Although he was named after a brave American Indian leader, Sherman believed the natives were an inferior people that would eventually be defeated after all their lands were occupied by U.S. citizens. *Above*, Sherman *(fourth from right, facing camera)* meets with Sioux leaders to negotiate a peace treaty.

approach. Congress, however, pushed for a more rigorous policy—one that would give African Americans a significant role in Southern politics. As the contest grew more tense, the army was drawn into the political fray. Sherman sided with the president. Johnson offered Sherman the position of secretary of war despite the fact that Edwin Stanton still had the job. Sherman had no desire for a civilian office, however. The president then offered the position to Ulysses S. Grant, but Grant also turned him down.

In January 1866, Ellen Sherman gave birth to another son. The Shermans christened him Philemon Tecumseh and called him "Cump," like his father. Sherman must have been thrilled to have another son. His son Charles, born in June of 1864, had died of a lung illness in December of that year, shortly after Sherman's capture of Savannah. Sherman grieved deeply for the loss of the son he never even saw.

In Washington, D.C., the political situation grew tenser. President Johnson was entangled in a power struggle with Congress and Secretary of War Stanton that centered on Reconstruction policies. The president had an intense desire to heal the wounds of war and quickly restore the Union. Many congressmen, however, wanted to punish the South. The Republicans in Congress strenuously opposed the mild Reconstruction policies of the Democratic President Johnson—policies that left political control in the hands of Southern whites. After taking an oath of loyalty to the Union, former Rebels were pardoned and were free to reestablish their civil government. This process guaranteed that African Americans in the South remained in an inferior status. When Congress tried to stiffen Reconstruction policies, Johnson grew stubborn. Eventually, Congress enacted laws that took away powers granted to the president by the Constitution, thereby giving Congress the upper hand.

The South was divided into five military districts, each one under the command of a Union general. As a price for readmission to the Union, each Southern state was required to call a constitutional convention to create a new state constitution. These constitutions had to guarantee voting rights for African Americans. Each state also had to ratify the

Fourteenth Amendment to the Constitution, which declared African Americans citizens. Once a state ratified the amendment, it could apply for readmission. After a state was approved and readmitted to the Union, Congress ended military rule, withdrew the troops from the state, and allowed senators and congressmen from the state back into Congress.

President Johnson still found ways to sidestep the new laws of Congress. In a final showdown, radicals in Congress tried to oust the president from office. In 1868, Congress moved to impeach Johnson. Although Johnson survived the critical vote, his days in office were numbered. In the 1868 presidential election, the Republicans chose Ulysses S. Grant as their candidate. In November, the voters handed Grant a sweeping victory.

With Grant as president, Sherman was up for a promotion. He already had succeeded Grant as lieutenant general in 1866. He now became a full general, as well as commanding general of the entire army. The promotion required Sherman to spend time in Washington. For a while, he considered turning down the offer because of the cost of moving. Fortunately, a group of wealthy businessmen offered to buy a fine house on I Street from Grant and present it to the new commanding general as a gift. The Shermans graciously accepted and prepared for another move.

COMMANDING GENERAL

As commanding general, Sherman found himself in a legal and administrative jungle. Since 1821, the army command had had three central elements: the commanding general, the secretary of war, and the general staff. Although these elements had been functioning together for almost half a century, the responsibilities and authorities of each of the three had never been clearly outlined. When Grant's secretary of war, John Rawlins, died in September 1869, Sherman suggested that Grant replace him with William Worth Belknap, an Iowa lawyer who had fought at Shiloh and rose to command a division under Sherman. Grant agreed.

Unfortunately, relations between Sherman and Belknap quickly deteriorated. Hard-driving and aggressive, Belknap issued orders directly to the army, bypassing Sherman entirely. Belknap also intruded on matters usually set aside for the commanding general, such as the running of West Point. Frustrated, Sherman asked President Grant to intervene. Grant sidestepped Sherman's request, however, and Sherman felt abandoned by his old commander.

Sherman's power continued to decline. In January 1870, John A. Logan, the chairman of the House Military Affairs Committee, introduced a bill that called for massive cuts in funding for the army. Logan moved to get rid of the regular army and rely, instead, on state militias and volunteer soldiers. He also aimed a shot at the commanding general. He pointed out that Sherman's salary of $19,000 was too high and proposed to eliminate the position of commanding general altogether. Sherman was sitting in the gallery of the House chamber that day, and he stormed out in a rage. A much-altered version of Logan's bill passed both the House and the Senate. The legislation made minor cuts in the army but major cuts in Sherman's pay.

In the fall of 1871, Sherman made a move he never would have made in war. He temporarily abandoned the field, leaving the enemy—Congress—to do as it wished. Admiral James Alden invited Sherman to join the navy's Atlantic Squadron on a cruise of the Mediterranean. He set sail in November. The itinerary took Sherman through the Mediterranean, to Turkey and Russia, and on a tour of European cities. At 51 years old, he climbed the 300-foot pyramid of Cheops, in Egypt. During the 10-month trip, he visited with various heads of state, from Great Britain's Queen Victoria to Saudi Arabia's Sultan Abdul Aziz. He walked over old battlefields and toured fortresses.

When Sherman returned to Washington, little had changed. Throughout the 1870s, he presided over the army's efforts to vanquish the American Indians or force them onto reservations. During this time, Sherman also worked to build up the army to a force of nearly 200,000 men. By the end of the decade, his job, for the most part, was completed.

SHERMAN'S FINAL DAYS

Sherman served as commanding general of the U.S. Army until 1884. It was his last and longest assignment. Although the promotion put him at the pinnacle of the army pyramid, it was not the peak of his career. The post carried far less power and prestige than that of the present-day army chief of staff. Also, the job thrust him into a world of high politics. It was a world in which he never could feel at home or move with the confidence and mastery he had known in the field. On February 8, 1884, President Chester A. Arthur issued the formal order of Sherman's retirement, bringing his military career to an end. On that day, the order was read aloud at evening parade to the officers and men at every army installation in the country. Sherman's life in retirement began on his sixty-fourth birthday.

In 1886, William and Ellen Sherman decided to move from their home in St. Louis to New York City. Ellen's health began to deteriorate rapidly. She suffered from shortness of breath and swollen feet—symptoms of circulatory disease. On November 28, 1888, Sherman was reading in his office when Ellen's nurse called down that his wife was dying. He raced up two flights of stairs, calling, "Ellen, wait for me!" By the time he reached her bedside, however, she had passed away.

On February 4, 1891, Sherman went out in bad weather to join a group at New York's Casino Theater. The next morning, he awoke with the symptoms of a cold. He got up, handled some paperwork, and went out to a wedding. On February 8, his seventy-first birthday, he fell ill with pneumonia. The

After a lifetime of military service, General William Tecumseh Sherman's distinguished career ended with a presidential order to retire from duty. Famous for his effective war strategies and determination in battle, Sherman is forever associated with bringing the Confederacy to its knees and the Civil War to an end.

Sherman children received telegrams instructing them to hurry to his bedside. As his condition worsened, he drifted in and out of consciousness.

In his moments of awareness, Sherman realized that he was dying. With his final breaths, he devised his own epitaph, which he kept repeating over and over. "Faithful and honorable," he whispered. On February 14, 1891, at 1:50 in the afternoon, Sherman died.

Sherman had wanted his funeral to be a simple military one. The nation would not have it that way, however. For 30 years, Sherman had been in the spotlight. Now, he had taken his place in the history books. There was much to remember: the military instructor in Louisiana who proclaimed his loyalty to the Union; the accusations of insanity; his redemption at Shiloh; the burning of Atlanta; and the dramatic success of his March to the Sea—the accomplishment that etched his name in American history.

The funeral service in New York City was a private one, but the procession that took his body to the funeral train was attended by tens of thousands of people who wanted to pay their last respects to the great hero of the Civil War. As Sherman's flag-draped casket rolled by, the tapping of drums and the tolling of bells filled the air. Behind the casket followed a riderless horse. From a railroad terminal in New Jersey, the general made a final journey to St. Louis, where he was laid to rest in Calvary Cemetery.

⚔ CHRONOLOGY ⚔

1820   Tecumseh Sherman is born on February 8 in
Lancaster, Ohio, to Charles Robert Sherman and
Mary Hoyt Sherman.

1829   Father dies from typhoid fever on June 24; due to
his mother's lack of money, Tecumseh goes to live at
the home of close friends and neighbors Maria and
Thomas Ewing.

1830   Baptized William by a Roman Catholic priest, name
changed to William T. Sherman.

1836   Enters the U.S. Military Academy at West Point, New
York, in June.

1840   Graduates from West Point sixth of 43 in his class;
reports for duty at Governor's Island, New York, in
September and is assigned to Fort Pierce, Florida.

1842   Company G is transferred to Fort Morgan, Mobile,
Alabama, in February.

1846   Congress declares war against Mexico, May 11–12;
ordered to join Company F of the 3rd Artillery
Regiment, assigned to California; leaves on July 14.

1848   Gold is discovered at Sutter's Mill, in California;
Mexican War ends in August.

1850   Marries Ellen Ewing on the evening of May 1;
ordered to report to Company C, 3rd Artillery,
commanded by Captain Braxton Bragg, at Jefferson
Barracks near St. Louis, Missouri; becomes captain in
the Commissary Corps; Ellen, who is pregnant, stays
with her family in Lancaster.

1851 Daughter Maria ("Minnie") Ewing Sherman is born on January 28; Ellen and Minnie join Sherman in St. Louis.

1852 Moves briefly to Fort Leavenworth, Kansas; Ellen, pregnant again, returns to Lancaster; ordered in August to become the commissary officer at New Orleans; mother dies on September 23; moves to New Orleans; daughter Mary Elizabeth ("Lizzie") born on November 17.

1853 Ellen and children arrive in New Orleans on January 1; Henry S. Turner offers Sherman the position of manager of Lucas, Turner, and Company, a new bank in San Francisco; Ellen and the girls return

TIMELINE

1850
Marries Ellen Ewing on the evening of May 1; becomes captain in the Commissary Corps

1820
Tecumseh Sherman is born on February 8 in Lancaster, Ohio

1853
Becomes manager of Lucas, Turner & and Company

1857
Lucas and Turner's bank closes, and the Shermans move to New York

1820

1830
Baptized William by a Roman Catholic priest, name changed to William T. Sherman

1860

1860
Becomes superintendent and engineering professor at the Louisiana Seminary of Learning and Military Academy; South Carolina secedes from the Union on December 24

1836
Enters the U.S. Military Academy at West Point, New York, in June

1840
Graduates from West Point sixth of 43 in his class; assigned to Fort Pierce, Florida

to Lancaster in February; Sherman leaves for San Francisco in March; Ellen and Lizzie join him in mid-October.

1854 Son William Ewing Sherman born on June 8.

1856 Son Thomas Ewing Sherman born on October 12.

1857 Lucas and Turner close the bank in San Francisco; Sherman and his family set sail for New York on May 20.

1859 Daughter Eleanor Mary ("Ellie") born on September 5.

1860 Becomes superintendent and professor of engineering at the Louisiana Seminary of Learning and Military

1861
Commands his brigade in the first battle of Bull Run on July 21; later suspected of insanity

1864-1865
Begins his Atlanta Campaign on May 7; begins famous March to the Sea on November 16; General Robert E. Lee surrenders to Ulysses S. Grant on April 12, bringing an end to the Civil War

1884
Retires from the army

1861

1891

1862
Assumes command of the Fifth Division of the Army of the Tennessee; regains his confidence and respect as a commander in the battle of Shiloh

1868
Becomes the commanding general of the United States Army

1891
Dies of pneumonia at the age of 71

1863
Vicksburg, Mississippi, falls to Union forces on July 4; Sherman is promoted to brigadier general

Academy; South Carolina secedes from the Union on December 24.

1861 Louisiana secedes from the Union on January 26; Sherman returns to Lancaster; becomes colonel of the 13th U.S. Infantry; daughter Rachel born on July 5; commands his brigade in the first battle of Bull Run on July 21; ordered to serve in Kentucky in August; asks to be relieved of command in Kentucky and is replaced by Brigadier General Don Carlos Buell; reports for duty under Major General Henry W. Halleck, commander of the Department of the Missouri in St. Louis; Sherman, mentally exhausted, takes a brief leave in Lancaster; is suspected of insanity.

1862 Assumes command of the Fifth Division of the Army of the Tennessee on March 1; regains his confidence and respect as a commander in the battle of Shiloh on April 6–7; fails in an attempt to capture Vicksburg in December.

1863 Vicksburg, Mississippi, falls to Union forces on July 4; Sherman is promoted to brigadier general; son Willie contracts typhoid fever and dies in Memphis on October 3; Union forces successfully fight off Rebels at Chattanooga in November.

1864 Begins his Atlanta campaign on May 7; son Charles Celestine born on June 11; begins famous March to the Sea on November 16; reaches Savannah on December 10; infant son Charles dies in December.

1865 In January, begins a second march through the Carolinas, leaving behind a massive line of fire and destruction; enters Columbia, South Carolina, on February 17; heads through North Carolina; Confederate general Robert E. Lee surrenders to

Union general Ulysses S. Grant on April 12, bringing an end to the Civil War.

1866 Promoted to lieutenant general and put in command of the Division of the Missouri.

1867 Son Philemon Tecumseh ("Cump") born on January 9.

1868 Becomes the commanding general of the United States Army.

1870s Commands the U.S. Army in the Indian Wars.

1884 Retires from the army on February 8.

1888 Ellen dies on November 28.

1891 Sherman dies of pneumonia on February 14, at the age of 71.

GLOSSARY

abolish To end.

abolitionist Someone who opposes slavery and works to end it.

adjutant Military staff officer who assists the commanding officer.

annex To add to something larger.

artillery Mounted guns, such as cannon.

battalion A tactical military unit that forms part of a division.

big guns Heavy artillery, such as cannon.

bombardment An attack with artillery.

campaign A series of military operations designed to reach a single goal.

casemates Armored enclosures for big guns.

casualties Those who are wounded, killed, or captured in a battle.

circuit court A court that holds sessions in various places within a district.

commissary An army officer in charge of supplies.

commodity Something of value that is bought and sold.

contraband Smuggled goods.

demerit A mark against a student for poor conduct or poor grades.

emancipation The act of freeing someone.

entrench To surround with ditches, or trenches.

flank The left or right side of a military formation.

garrison A military post or station.

idiosyncrasies Quirks or odd behaviors.

infantry Foot soldiers.

insurrection   Rebellion.

ironclad   In the Civil War, a ship covered with iron plating for protection.

levee   An embankment built to prevent a river from flooding the surrounding land.

nonperishable   Word used to describe a food item that keeps for a long time.

parade   An organized march for display.

plebe   A military trainee; at West Point, a first-year student.

rank   In the military, a certain position.

regiment   A military unit smaller than a division.

repeal   To revoke or cancel.

reveille   A signal on a bugle or drum in the morning to wake soldiers.

run (on a bank)   A rush by many customers to take their money out of a bank when they fear that the bank may go out of business and their money may be lost.

secede   To withdraw.

slave codes   State laws that defined the status of slaves and the rights of slave owners.

surveyor   Someone who describes, measures, and documents areas of land.

sympathizer   Someone who supports a certain cause.

transport   A boat or ship used to move troops.

BIBLIOGRAPHY

Bailey, Anne J. *The Chessboard of War: Sherman and Hood in the Autumn Campaigns of 1864*. Lincoln: University of Nebraska Press, 2000.

Coburn, Mark. *Terrible Innocence: General Sherman at War*. New York: Hippocrene Books, 1993.

Davis, Burke. *Sherman's March*. New York: Random House, 1980.

Fellman, Michael. *Citizen Sherman*. New York: Random House, 1995.

Flood, Charles Bracelen. *Grant and Sherman: The Friendship that Won the Civil War*. New York: Farrar, Straus and Giroux, 2005.

Glatthaar, Joseph T. *The March to the Sea and Beyond: Sherman's Troops in the Savannah and Carolinas Campaigns*. New York: New York University Press, 1985.

Hirshson, Stanley P. *The White Tecumseh*. New York: John Wiley & Sons, Inc., 1997.

Kennett, Lee. *Sherman: A Soldier's Life*. New York: Harper-Collins, 2001.

McDonough, James Lee, and James Pickett Jones. *War So Terrible: Sherman and Atlanta*. New York: W.W. Norton & Company, 1987.

Merrill, James M. *William Tecumseh Sherman*. New York: Rand McNally & Company, 1971.

Miers, Earl Schenck. *The General Who Marched to Hell*. New York: Dorset Press, 1951.

Sherman, William Tecumseh. *Memoirs of General W.T. Sherman.* New York: Literary Classics of the United States, 1990.

Simpson, Brooks D., and Jean V. Berlin, eds. *Sherman's Civil War: Selected Correspondence of William T. Sherman, 1860–1865.* Chapel Hill: University of North Carolina Press, 1999.

 FURTHER RESOURCES

BOOKS

Aretha, David. *Jefferson Davis*. New York: Chelsea House, 2008.

Crompton, Samuel Willard. *Ulysses S. Grant*. New York: Chelsea House, 2008.

Hyslop, Steve. *Eyewitness to the Civil War*. Washington, D.C.: National Geographic, 2006.

Koestler-Grack, Rachel A. *Stonewall Jackson*. New York: Chelsea House, 2008.

McNeese, Tim. *The Abolitionist Movement: Ending Slavery*. New York: Chelsea House, 2007.

———. *The Emancipation Proclamation: Ending Slavery in America*. New York: Chelsea House, 2008.

———. *Robert E. Lee*. New York: Chelsea House, 2008.

Ray, Delia. *Behind the Blue & Gray: The Soldier's Life in the Civil War*. New York: Lodestar Books, 1991.

Sonneborn, Liz. *Harriet Beecher Stowe*. New York: Chelsea House, 2008.

Sterngass, Jon. *John Brown*. New York: Chelsea House, 2008.

Wagner, Heather Lehr. *The Outbreak of the Civil War: A Nation Tears Apart*. New York: Chelsea House, 2008.

WEB SITES

The American Civil War
www.theamericancivilwar.com

CivilWar.com: the Home of the Civil War
  http://www.civilwar.com

The Civil War: A Film by Ken Burns, at PBS
  http://www.pbs.org/civilwar

PICTURE CREDITS

PAGE

INDEX

145

 ABOUT THE AUTHOR

RACHEL A. KOESTLER-GRACK has worked on nonfiction books as an editor and writer since 1999. During her career, she has dealt with historical topics that range from the Middle Ages, to America's colonial era, to the years of the civil rights movement. In addition, she has written numerous biographies of a variety of historical and contemporary figures. She lives with her husband and daughter in the German community of New Ulm, Minnesota.